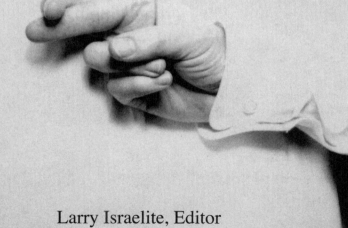

LIES
ABOUT
LEARNING

Leading Executives
Separate Truth from Fiction
In a $100 Billion Industry

Larry Israelite, Editor

ASTD Press is an internationally renowned source of insightful and practical information on workplace learning and performance topics, including training basics, evaluation and return-on-investment (ROI), instructional systems development (ISD), e-learning, leadership, and career development.

Ordering information: Books published by ASTD Press can be purchased by visiting our website at store.astd.org or by calling 800.628.2783 or 703.683.8100.

Library of Congress Control Number: 2006932459

ISBN-10: 1-56286-454-8
ISBN-13: 978-1-56286-454-5

Manager, Acquisitions and Author Development: Mark Morrow
Editorial Manager: Jacqueline Edlund-Braun
Editorial Assistant: Kelly Norris
Copyeditor: Karen Eddleman
Indexer: April Davis
Interior Design and Production: Kathleen Schaner
Cover Design: Liz Jones
Cover Illustration: Adam Mitchinson

Printed by Victor Graphics, Inc., Baltimore, Maryland, www.victorgraphics.com.

➤ Contents

➤ **Preface**

In the late 1990s, I used to receive frequent phone calls from suppliers of enterprise learning management systems. Most of them sounded the same to me—some introductory comments, a quick reading of the learning tea leaves, and then the pitch. Most of these calls were uninspiring but pleasant. One company, however, used a pitch that was, shall I say, a little unconventional and very aggressive. I would answer the phone and hear someone shouting something like this: "This is John Smith from [fill in your own catchy Internet-era company name]. Do you know that e-learning will comprise 90 percent of the training offered in your organization within the next two years and that your chief executive officer will *demand* to see detailed training reports for all of your employees on a regular basis?" (I would often hear John's fist pounding on a desk in the background as he delivered this warning.)

I would politely say, "No, it won't, and no, he won't" and then try to hang up. But, before I could even remove the phone from my ear, the enthusiastic sales consultant would berate me for not accepting my responsibility as a learning leader and, I think, yell something about a curse of one sort or another on my children. I never bought anything from this supplier, but many others did, not only from this company but from many others like it.

In fact, a great deal of money was spent on a variety of complex systems that were supposed to be able to track the vast amount of e-learning that would be delivered on practically every subject known to humankind. Some funny things happened on the way to this digital forum, however. First, classroom programs didn't disappear, and, unfortunately, most learning management systems were not well suited for managing anything except e-learning. Second, as it turned out, all the large e-learning course catalogs that neatly populated learning management systems and on which many companies spent even more money were never really used all that much. In the end, learning managers scratched their heads and wondered what had happened; they had spent plenty of money but had little to show for it.

Was this an isolated incident? Was this the first time that a new approach to learning or some new technology captured the imaginations of those involved in corporate learning to such an extent that their irrational exuberance caused them to ignore that little voice in their heads that kept telling them to "slow down." I wish the answer were yes. I wish the lure of e-learning and learning management systems were so far beyond anything that learning professionals had experienced that they momentarily lost their senses. Unfortunately, this just isn't the case. The road we in the learning profession travel is littered with expensive failed experiments, unfulfilled promises, unachieved goals, and frustrating disappointments.

Now, don't panic! I am not saying (or implying) that those who are the custodians of the corporate schoolhouse have not enjoyed tremendous success, as measured in satisfied learners, improved business performance, seats at the table, the respect of business leaders, and other equally significant metrics. What I am saying, however, is that there have been a few errors along the way. The biggest mistake, however, may be the failure to identify, evaluate, and learn from those errors.

I should mention here that the need to find simple solutions to big problems is not isolated to the learning professional. I have tried a few fad diets. (No smart comments please! That's why I have a wife and children!) I have bought, repurposed, and sold all sorts of exercise equipment over my lifetime. I have even responded to the odd—and I do mean odd—infomercial from time to time, all in my quest to reduce some burden that I believe I am carrying. Guess what? I don't weigh any less, I am in no better shape, and, well, let's just say that it was only a small fire that we were able to contain and extinguish quickly. The pressure to find quick fixes is almost universal, and this pressure makes people believe things they shouldn't believe and do things they shouldn't do.

Exposing the Lies About Learning

This book sheds some light on the hype—the lies—about learning that are spread by product marketing literature, training association conference presentations, and pronouncements by industry pundits. What do I mean by lies? I mean conventional wisdom, self-serving rumors, and unfounded insinuations. I mean all of the data and information that learning professionals and executives encounter as they try to make basic decisions about the strategies and tactics of corporate learning.

So are they really lies? Do I really believe that there is rampant deceit in the learning industry? Am I that cynical? People who know me well probably would tell you that I am about as cynical as anyone who has been around for a while. Although I don't think that most people deliberately attempt to deceive, I think there is rampant over-optimism about the new products, tools, and technologies that we hear about every single day. When something works in one situation, learning professionals desperately want to believe it will work in all situations. When a success is achieved with one population, success is expected with all populations. When a new product possesses technical capabilities that could lead to a desirable result, trainers accept without evidence that the result will be achieved. And, in all of these cases, it is too easy to commit resources, promise results, and in other ways put personal and organizational credibility on the line.

Why do learning professionals do this? Everyone is on a quest for the holy grail of learning—the one product, process, program, or promise that will allow them to dramatically improve the quantity, quality, and impact of learning in their respective organizations and to do this faster and cheaper than ever before. Because of this intense desire, learning professionals are willing to believe almost anything; they willingly, even enthusiastically, fall victim to some or all of the lies about learning.

Just in case you were thinking this is all about technology, you are wrong. That would be too simple. It is tempting to believe all sorts of things in the name of better, faster, and cheaper solutions to persistent problems. Technology is only one piece of the puzzle. There are many more.

One of the challenges faced by most editors (and authors, for that matter) is how to choose content. In this case, the problem was to select the lies that would make for the most interesting and helpful reading. I would like to tell you that there was some science behind the selection process, but there wasn't. I simply chose the topics that I hear my colleagues talking about at conferences, in meetings, and in personal conversations. Learning professionals worry about their customers, the products they deliver to them, and their careers. In one form or another, all of the chapters touch one or more of these topics.

How Can This Book Help You?

The purpose of this book is to explore the most common lies about learning and then to offer some practical tips about how to deal with them. My goal, and the goal of all the book's contributors, is to provide business executives and learning professionals with enough ammunition to ask the right questions, kick the right tires, and maintain the right level of skepticism about what they read and hear about learning products, tools, and technologies as they pursue their goals. You need to be able to make prudent decisions that lead to measurable, predictable, meaningful results.

I hope you will find something useful in these pages and that something you read here might enable you to make your way through the maze of corporate learning with a little less resistance and with fewer wrong turns. If this book helps you to do that, then we will have created something of value.

Additionally, one of my goals is to create a community in which more lies can be identified and discussed. If you would like to share some of your own lies about learning, please send them to LiesAboutLearning@gmail.com or visit the Lies About Learning blog at http://liesaboutlearning.blogspot.com/.

Acknowledgments

I am extremely grateful to many people for making this book possible in their own unique but incredibly important ways:

- ➤ The 11 authors, who generously contributed their knowledge, experience, and time in the preparation and ongoing refinement of their chapters
- ➤ Tina Busch, whose ideas, insights, and advice are always useful and greatly appreciated
- ➤ Lou and Jim Carey, who have been my teachers, mentors, and friends since I first ventured into the world of learning almost 30 years ago
- ➤ And, most important, my family, whose love, understanding, support, tolerance, and sense of humor sustain me each and every day.

Royalties from this book will be donated to SoundWaters, a non-profit organization based in Stamford, Connecticut, whose mission is to protect the Long Island Sound through education. SoundWaters offers a wide array of educational opportunities for students from kindergarten to college. Programs are offered aboard the schooner *SoundWaters,* at the SoundWaters Community Center for Environmental Education, and at classrooms and field sites throughout southern Connecticut. See www.soundwaters.org for additional information.

Larry Israelite
September 2006

An Extended Table of Contents

Larry Israelite

One of the raging debates in learning circles is how to measure the utilization of e-learning. Traditionally, program completion has been one of the key metrics for learning activities: Did someone go through a program from start to finish? In a classroom setting, this makes sense; but in an e-world, it may not. Technology allows learners to look at the outline of a learning activity, make judgments about the topics that really matter, and then go through them. There is no compulsion to complete. Rather, there is a compulsion to get what is needed when it is needed. In other words, it is just-enough, just-in-time learning.

Other media function the same way. People scan newspapers to find the stories they want to read or skip over songs they don't like on CDs. Likewise, most readers browse a book's table of contents to find the chapters that pique their interest. Unfortunately, chapter titles don't always contain enough information to be useful. What is really needed is a couple of paragraphs that explain the chapter content in some detail. That's what you will find in this chapter. The goal is to help you find the information you need just before you need it.

Chapter 2: Lies About Learners

Learners, after all, are the final element of what can be a fairly complicated customer value chain. Why not just call them customers? Think about it: You can have any number of customers, including a sponsor, a funder, a buyer, a trainer, a manager, and, finally, a learner. The learner, in certain situations, is just one of a series of stakeholders whose needs have to be addressed. However, the learner is the person for whom training, job aids, or other forms of learning interventions are designed. And learners can be complex characters.

There is a fair amount of conventional wisdom about learners these days. This wisdom focuses on diversity in the broadest sense of the word: race, gender, age, education, and learning style, just to name a few. The problem is that almost everyone has a thing or two to say about how to approach these differences. In his chapter, Murry Christensen explores some of the incorrect assumptions made about learners and how these influence the learning products created on their behalf.

Chapter 3: Lies About the Design of Learning

I am an instructional designer and proud of it. I went to graduate school, earned a doctoral degree, and spent more than 20 years practicing my craft or managing others who do the same. I am continually amazed at how many people feel compelled to stand up at conferences and announce my imminent demise and that of all the other instructional designers. I can accept that from my children, who remind me all too frequently of my obsolescence, but not from complete strangers who often don't really understand what trained, competent instructional designers know, think, or are capable of contributing to the creation of effective learning and the improvement of business performance.

Why does this happen? I think there are a few reasons. First, most people don't realize the amount of science that supports the art of learning design. Consequently, they live with the misconceptions that design doesn't matter much to begin with or, if it does matter, that anyone can do it. Second, and more insidiously, people can be seduced by technologies that support the distribution or delivery of learning. Whether it's video, CD-ROMs, the Internet, or gaming devices, there is an assumption that the professionals who produce the media are all that is required to create good learning. Unfortunately, this never works, and instructional designers live to see another day. In this chapter, Melinda Jackson describes and debunks the standard set of myths that lead to the mistaken belief that the art and science of instructional design simply aren't necessary.

Chapter 4: Lies About Careers in Learning

There may be no organization in major corporations that has as diverse a workforce as the training organization. I am not, in this context, referring to the same types of diversity Murry Christensen describes in chapter 2 or what one typically means when using that term. Instead, I mean the variety of educational and professional backgrounds of the individuals who make up current-day training organizations. Some have technical and professional degrees, and others have no degree at all. Training professionals come from all parts of the business—sales, marketing, engineering, manufacturing, or finance. They are teachers, programmers, designers, and subject matter experts. Some are intentional learning professionals and others are here by accident; they took an unexpected or involuntary turn on the career highway. Many learning professionals have questioned whether their profession will provide the long-term career opportunities they seek. Others question whether learning is a career at all.

In her discussion about lies about careers in learning, Beth Thomas directly confronts the assumptions made about having (or not having) successful learning careers. At the same time, she celebrates the opportunities learning professionals have for making a real difference to their customers and for creating exciting options for ongoing, long-term professional growth and development.

Chapter 5: Lies About Chief Learning Officers

A few years ago—okay, more than a few—learning professionals began to dabble in organizational and job title changes as a means of changing perceptions of the value of the products and services they provided to customers. Training associates became training consultants who became learning consultants or performance consultants. Training and development organizations became learning and development organizations or even learning services. It wasn't clear that the work changed all that much or that any more value was delivered, but there was a noticeable improvement in collective self-image. After all, "learning" and "performance" are such inspirational words, and "training" is so mundane!

Learning professionals, however, weren't the only ones playing in the job title sandbox. Suddenly, a title of vice president just didn't have sufficient gravitas in organizations, and chiefs began to appear with astonishing frequency (or reckless abandon)—chief information officers, chief financial officers, chief marketing officers, chief e-business officers, and, last, but not least, chief learning officers. At this point, it isn't clear if this title change has led to a change in perceptions about the value of learning, but Len Sherman provides us with a sobering perspective on the challenges learning professionals must surmount to make the word "chief" into more than just a transitory title.

Chapter 6: Lies About Learning Consultants

Corporate learning functions could not exist without external learning consultants and vendors. Simply put, one can't have on staff a sufficient number of resources with the skills required to manage the demands of internal customers. As Edward Trolley points out in chapter 7, a variable resource strategy is a key requirement for effective management of the learning function within an organization. At the same time, the learning consulting industry wouldn't exist if there weren't a need for the kinds of products and services it offers to its corporate clients. You would think that, given this mutual need, everyone would get along, right? Well, think again.

For reasons that don't always make sense and are never completely logical, the relationships between consultants and their clients are often strained. Charlene Zeiberg, who has experience on all sides of this issue, having worked as a consultant for a well-known training vendor and as a member of a corporate training function, provides a comprehensive review of what can go wrong in these complex relationships and how to prevent it.

Chapter 7: Lies About Managing the Learning Function

For as long as I can remember one of the key criticisms of training managers is that they think training is what they actually manage. This is not true, and training managers should not be under the impression that it's all they do. To be successful, they have to take a much broader view of their roles. Twenty years ago, the narrower view might have been OK. It isn't any more, and those of us in the learning profession who don't get this should engage in career counseling pronto.

Why the change? At the risk of answering a complex question with a very short answer, the reason is that the business environment has changed. Organizations have fewer human resources, less money, increased competition, and almost unbelievable scrutiny, thanks to the Sarbanes-Oxley Act. Every budget is studied, every expense analyzed, every request for resources, human or otherwise, is evaluated, manipulated, and, more often than not, rejected. Training organizations are under a microscope. Often, they are viewed with the same suspicion as other overhead functions, which are candidates for reducing, outsourcing, or eliminating altogether. Yikes!

In this chapter, Edward Trolley contends that learning leaders have to become business leaders who think and act as business people and who are held to rigid, business-related metrics. The lies he discusses represent the things learning professionals often tell themselves (or are told by others) to justify their existence and their inclination to maintain the status quo.

Chapter 8: Lies About E-Learning

There are some truths about lies. For example, the bigger the lie, the more effective it is. The longer you tell the lie, the more likely it is to be believed. A composite lie, which I define as one big lie comprising several little, seemingly unrelated, yet quite plausible lies, is preferable to and has more apparent veracity than a single lie about one topic or issue. Finally, lies that are told many times in front of a large number of people are far more easily believed than lies that are told in private. Such are the lies about e-learning.

There are some truths about lies. For example, the bigger the lie, the more effective it is. The longer you tell the lie, the more likely it is to be believed.

The odd thing about e-learning lies is that they never change, and, ironically, they often aren't even about e-learning. Rather, they are about many of the other lies addressed in this book. Learners like it because it's easier to manage, it's easier to design and develop, it's more effective, it tastes great, it's less filling...the list goes on. No one understands all of this better than Elliott Masie, who offers his unique perspective on struggles with what most people agree should no longer be a source of ongoing frustration and aggravation.

Chapter 9: Lies About Learning Technology Tools

I used to attend the annual conference of a professional association devoted solely to learning technology. Most of the sessions were delivered by employees of technology vendors who often used this conference to introduce new products and services to working learning professionals. Conference attendees were mesmerized with the talk of a fabulous future, replete with tools and technologies that would single-handedly solve all those pesky learning problems that confronted them daily.

After a few years, however, it began to sound all too familiar. It seemed as though the presentations were the same year after year; all that changed were the names of the products and services. I still have a memory of one presenter who every year delivered a keynote address during which he assured the audience that this year was different, that this time [insert product name here] was really going to fix [insert your favorite learning problem here]. Boy, was he good! Of course, nothing ever turned out the way we were led to believe it would. Yet, regular attendees like me went back to that conference, deeply wanting to believe that this year would be different. It never was. In his chapter, J.P. Lacombe explores the statements that are made about learning technologies that will continue to get learning professionals into all sorts of trouble even though they really ought to know better.

Chapter 10: Lies About Learning to Lead

No one argues too much about the training delivered by learning professionals in an organization. People have opinions about it: how it ought to be designed, which combination of media should be used to deliver it, and how it should be measured, for example. But, for the most part, you don't hear too many discussions about whether a particular subject matter or topic can be taught or learned. Such is not the case with leadership. Many think that leadership is an innate capability that, at best, can be uncovered, but certainly not created if it is not present in the first place.

On the other hand, the issue of leadership development is at or near the top of almost every list of the challenges facing current business leaders. There is an entire industry built around the design and delivery of leadership training. So innate or learnable, teachable or not, a great deal of energy and even more money are expended trying to help people learn to lead. In this chapter, Kerry Johnson discusses what he describes as the hero myth of leadership and then presents an approach to teaching leaders that is distinctly different from more traditional teaching techniques.

Chapter 11: Lies About Learning Organizations

It isn't enough that employees are supposed to learn. Now organizations are supposed to learn as well. Is a learning organization one in which there is a culture that values learning? Does that mean that there are investments in employee development and that employees who increase their capabilities and, therefore, their value to the company are rewarded for doing so? Or, is it possible for all of those things to be present in an organization that doesn't learn?

If this seems confusing, don't be alarmed. Many learning experts have tried to figure this one out for years, and each time they get close, it seems as though the rug is pulled out from under them. The truth is that I'm not sure anyone really understands it, with the possible exception of the consultants who make their livings trying to make it clear to the rest of us. As Steven Ober points out in his chapter, it isn't even certain that they really know what they are talking about.

Chapter 12: Lies About Research

"There are three types of lies: lies, damn lies, and statistics." This statement, often attributed to Mark Twain, although it may have been first uttered by Disraeli, summarizes the challenges of trying to read and interpret research about learning and all that surrounds it. The sad fact is that numbers can be manipulated to say almost most anything. (Just listen to the spin surrounding any political controversy!) I am not necessarily talking about formal academic research. People are inundated with definitive statements about the benefits of the products and services they hope will enable them to achieve their business goals. Unfortunately, they can't always trust the numbers they're given and should never believe everything they read!

David Stone's chapter doesn't describe any specific lies about research. Rather, it provides an approach, a method, and some tools to critically evaluate the information—the lies—encountered by learning professionals every day as they seek solutions to the critical problems faced by their clients.

Chapter 13: Final Thoughts: Some Truths About Learning

I used to know people who attended *est* seminars. I may still know some, but no one admits it quite as freely as they did 20 years ago. The only thing I remember about what anyone learned from their *est* experience was that they acknowledged that "they owned their own stuff." ("Stuff" wasn't the word they used, but it is the one I'm allowed to print here.) In other words, they accepted responsibility for the condition of their lives. In a few cases, they actually stopped whining about the things they were unhappy about and started making some meaningful changes in their lives. It was impressive.

Learning professionals must do the same thing: Accept the responsibility for the current state of their profession. The final chapter contains one person's perspective about the "stuff" learning professionals have to start owning up to and some concrete actions they must take to improve their current situations.

Onward!

It's possible, I suppose, that you read this chapter in its entirety, thus contradicting the "random access to information" theory on which it was based. If this is the case, I thank you for your diligence and your interest. If you decide to go through the chapters in the order in which they were written, I think you will find a somewhat natural order to everything. If, however, you decide to be more opportunistic and find the information you need just as you need it, that should work also. In either case, the key is to remember that only you know your environment—the clients you support, the business challenges they face, and the constraints under which you have to work. Consequently, I encourage you to view what you read in each chapter as a starting point. In the end, only you know how to use these lies and the corresponding truths to create good results for your customers, which is, after all, what everyone wants.

➤ 2

Lies About Learners

Murry Christensen

President Harry S. Truman once said he wanted an economist who was one-handed. Why? Because his economic advisors would typically give him economic advice stating, "On the one hand...and on the other..." (Thredgold, 2001).

It may seem like a bit of a jump to go from practicing economists to learners, but like everyone, every economist had to start somewhere. Anyone who has read economics will surely chuckle in recognition and appreciation at the anecdote, but the position itself isn't as unlikely as the joke makes it sound—a lot of jokes work that way. The world is a complex place, especially when you throw primates with opposable thumbs into the mix.

Although the search for a silver-bullet solution is understandable, the longer you work in the field, the more you realize the quest is bogus because there aren't any silver bullets, just hard work and careful thought. When you find what looks like single causation in human affairs you should be suspicious because it's probably a scam of some kind—maybe not as egregiously venal as an Enron, but there's likely to be something missing in the argument. This is certainly true in learning. Multiplying metaphors now, think about the little angel that perches on one shoulder and the little devil on the other, each whispering a seductive story in your ear. Isn't it interesting that the attribution as to which one controls all the details is given to both the divine and the diabolic (Hirsch, Kett, & Trefil, 2002)?

So, bear with me. In the spirit of rigorous inquiry, I'm going to play *advocatus diaboli* (devil's advocate), noting that in formal Catholic usage the role is also called—perhaps more trenchantly for this purpose—*Promotor Fidei,* meaning serving as guardian of the integrity of the process and promoter of the faith (*Catholic Encyclopedia,* 1907). This could go on for a very long time, so, for simplicity's sake, I've boiled the discussion down to four questions that seem particularly important:

> ➤ *Awareness:* How does the learner's sense of need influence learning?
> ➤ *Motivation:* What part do internal and external incentives play in learning?
> ➤ *Personalization:* How specific do learning professionals need to be to have a measurable effect?
> ➤ *Theory:* Should learning professionals worry about cognitive theories when building learning activities?

OK, here's my full disclosure, the fine print: Just because I started with a chirality shtick doesn't imply a right-left or red-blue valence. There has to be some respite from that conversation. No matter how my arguments sound, the basis is not politics, Sonny, just business. Oh, by the way, chirality is just a high-falutin' way of saying right-handed or left-handed. Feel free to drop it into conversations to impress people.

Awareness: Learners Don't Know What They Don't Know

On One Hand—Learners Need the Guidance of a Top-Down Learning Organization.

Learners don't know what they don't know. That's why companies have training groups. The orderly development of an organization's skill base requires planning, coordination, and judgment. Skills need to be coordinated with strategy, and strategy has to respond to changes in the larger business environment. Individuals can't reasonably be expected to know the larger picture. Ignoring this difference in perspective is a quick way to handicap the organization's ability to adjust to change in a coordinated manner.

Organizations aren't ant colonies, driven by instinctual imperatives. Organizations are made up of individuals who need support and guidance if they are to work in harmony for a greater good.

Removing or downgrading the central planning and support function would do a great disservice to every individual. People have enough to do keeping up with the current demands of their jobs. It's unfair—and dangerously stupid—to expect them to devote additional energy to thinking through and preparing for what's coming next. And, then if they get it wrong what happens? Does the victim get blamed?

People who've studied what's called knowledge management make a distinction between explicit knowledge, the possession of which is consciously apparent, and tacit knowledge, which is put to use but not consciously apparent to the individual employing it (Atherton, 2005). Management consultants and learning theorists have recast this distinction into a four-quadrant diagram, sometimes called the "don't know what you don't know" schema (figure 2-1).

Figure 2-1. Don't know what you don't know.

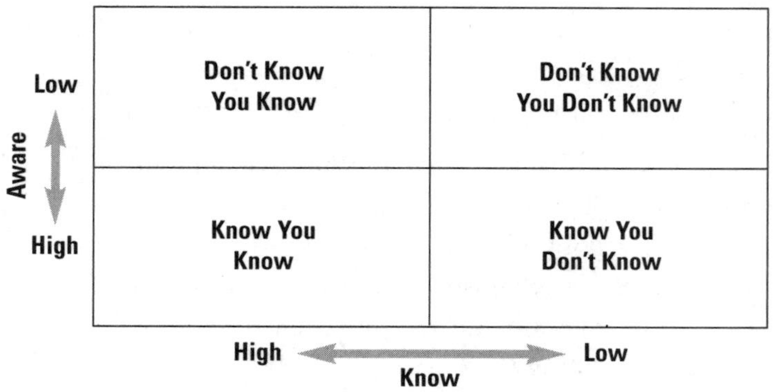

Expecting learners to autodidact is to ask them to come into possession of the upper right quadrant on their own, as if by magic. A bit of a stretch, don't you think, to assume that?

On the Other Hand—Learners Already Know What They Need to Know; We Training Professionals Just Have to Get Out of Their Way.

In today's rapidly evolving business environment, it's unreasonable— and probably foolish, if not dangerous—to leave staff development to some top-down process. It's important for training professionals to realize there's just too little time to let information about critical learning needs percolate down from corporate strategy, to group tactics, to individual skill needs on a case-by-case basis. It's better to publicize the overall strategy and then let smart people get on with it. After all, people are usually smarter than they're given credit for when they are treated like adults.

Besides, in today's flatter organizations the individual is much closer to the real problems than he or she ever used to be. The bureaucracy, driven by multiple constituencies and slow to react, is farther away from the issue. A modern business functions more like a federation of ever-shifting project teams. Groups that assemble for the duration of a specific project pick up skills they need on the fly and accomplish that task quite independently. The group then dissolves in preparation for the next project. In this flux-driven world, there's no way that a central learning organization can keep up. It's better to see the social contract governing that central function's role as one of providing resources, support, and incentives for self-directed learning (Christensen, 2005).

In this view, the learning organization can better spend its time:

➤ interpreting and communicating the development implications of current strategy

➤ developing a pool of resources suited to that direction

➤ creating access mechanisms, incentives, and infrastructure that help people find and use those resources

➤ guiding and tuning the ongoing process of self-development through individual initiatives.

Now, that's real value in modern business!

Motivation: Why Should They Care?

Argument From the Right Side—
People Don't Care About Learning, Just Results.

Although it sounds a bit cynical, the truth is that most people don't really care about learning, just results. People do what they're rewarded for doing. In a corporate setting, the word "results" usually means perform-ance review or compensation. Is this a surprise? Is there anything wrong if such is the case? The important issues are to first clarify the linkage between learning and reward, and then make the experience itself some-thing more attractive than dental work.

Really, why is the organization sponsoring the learning effort in the first place? It's not being done for some generalized social good. It's being done to advance the organization's self-interest. That's a simple, important fact.

When there's a disconnect, it lies in the lack of a consistent man-agement approach. First, a well-communicated and explicit linkage from strategy, through tactics, down to the individual's development program is critical. If you don't know, you can't act. Equally important, the second part of the solution is to have incentives that work in har-mony with that communication. When incentives are in place and implemented in a straightforward manner, the majority of people are more than prepared to take part.

The real problem comes when people's needs are underserved because management and the learning function fail to respond to an obvious need or, paradoxically, if their needs are overserved, as is hap-pening with the torrent of compliance training slathered on top of what is often an already full calendar.

Argument From the Left Side—Learners Take It on Trust That
a Learning Event Will Be a Valuable Experience.

Forget the "humans are learning machines" bit. Everybody knows that. (File this datum away under "Wisdom, Received.") More important, the past 15 years or so have taught most people that they have a vested career interest in learning and development. Learning professionals must make effective resources available in a way that learners can make the right choices about investing time and energy in the effort. Learning theories of various kinds say that unless barriers exist, people will learn. In fact, try to find a theory that argues that people don't want to learn.

If there's a problem, it's that the learning profession has too often

- ➤ been seduced by process rather than results
- ➤ failed to learn how to talk about the value of learning in terms that business leaders can properly value and integrate with strategy
- ➤ represented the learning function inadequately when incentive systems are put in place
- ➤ done a poor job of rising to the opportunity and trusting the learner to be a full partner in the development process.

Personalization: Who Are the Learners?

Point—Learners Are Essentially the Same.

Well, of course, they are. Time for the Homer Simpson "Doh!" award. The real question is: Does it matter? After all, people are all equipped with pretty much the same sensory equipment. Of course, some people have disabilities such as reduced hearing or vision problems or dyslexia, for example. Or, maybe English is not a learner's primary language, but there are delineated, often mandated, strategies for managing all these issues of accessibility.

All the talk about learning styles ratchets up the complexity, and there's no stopping point. Money, time, and energy are limited; there's just no point in obsessing over something like the difference between auditory and visual processing. Let's just get on with it!

Although advances in capability and reduction in cost have narrowed the differences in online delivery, the heterogeneity of platforms forces training professionals to focus on some reasonable lowest common denominator (LCD) implementations. Text and some reasonable level of graphics and animation are safe, everything else is a nice-to-have, not a must-have. Besides, the more learning professionals focus on multiple learning styles, the longer and more expensive development becomes, the higher the maintenance costs rise, and the difficulty in delivering the right learning activity to the right person increases. Besides, how many learning styles can learning professionals accommodate?

Focusing on first principles, it would be better to search for commonalities rather than differences. Though not always articulated, one of the tasks of a learning organization is to create a common culture in the organization. So is this accomplished by focusing, even implicitly, on things that set people apart? Or, would it be better to discharge responsibilities by identifying and supporting the things that people have in common and can bind them together?

In an ideal world, of course, each person would be treated as a unit of one, across any dimension you can define. Our world, however, is by no means ideal. The messy reality inhabited by learning professionals— especially in business—doesn't give them that luxury. Instead, learning professionals need to focus on identifying messages and tasks that make a crucial difference to the organization.

Counterpoint—Every Learner Is a Unique Individual.

Business drivers keep getting more complex and sophisticated, placing greater demands on both the program and the learner. Learning styles do make a significant difference in the results obtained, but it's necessary to start taking account of other important personal factors. What do individuals already know? What incentives are they reacting to? What's their work environment like? These factors have as much or more to do with the results as learning styles do. If the concern is about efficiency, treating everyone the same means aiming at the LCD. This, in turn, has two implications:

➤ A great deal of time is spent giving people things they already know.

➤ The dumbing down associated with an LCD effort means the opportunity to cultivate the better performers to their maximum potential is missed.

Perhaps a better way to spend one's time and energy is to think more carefully about what learners know and how their existing knowledge and skills can be usefully augmented, rather than worrying what modality should be used to reach them. As a wise man once said to me, "The most effective training you can deliver is the training you don't deliver." That truly is better, faster delivery.

Let's go back to the management consultant's four-quadrant diagram, but don't look at it from the "don't know what you don't know" perspective. Instead, use a lens of what the learner really needs to know given the reality of today's world. The axes transform from a knowledge/awareness orientation to one of time sensitivity/need to know, as shown in figure 2-2. This orientation helps shift attention from the general to the specific and closes the loop from theory to personalization.

Most important, designers begin to think about that oh-so-critical upper half of the diagram, which represents a pile of money in the center of the table doused with lighter fluid and set ablaze. Going back to the wise man mentioned previously, he'd also stress that "The cheapest training you can deliver is the training you don't deliver." And, it's risk-free to boot. When I worked in the printing business, the mantra was "Better, faster, cheaper. Pick any two." Of course, to identify that magic quadrant, learning professionals must treat each learner as an individual—at a minimum, as a definable segment—and then design accordingly.

Theory: How Do We Reach Them?

Heads, You Win—Younger Learners Are Inherently Different From Older Ones.

Are they? The hot trends in learning circles would have you believe so. On the one hand, this issue is really part of the larger discussion

Figure 2-2. What the learner really needs to know given the reality of today's world.

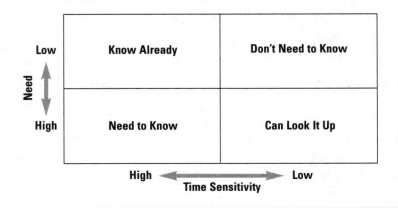

regarding learning personalization. On the other hand (there I go again!), enough people seem to think that the differences that revolve around age are substantial enough to warrant taking on the Millennial Learner issue all by itself.

There's an interesting paradox in the learning business. The majority of people doing research in academia and management in adult training settings are at least a generation older than the people about which they're busy making generalizations. They didn't grow up in the same and probably radically different world that a 20-year-old has—a world of instantaneous communication, flat hierarchy, saturation marketing, multiple gratifications, distrust of authority, and media convergence.

Both research and anecdotal evidence indicate that, to a degree unmatched by earlier age cohorts, the younger generations of learners are characterized by a demand for the following:

➤ relevant development activities
➤ rich experiences
➤ flexibility in scheduling
➤ community as a primary component
➤ technology emphasis and familiarity
➤ instant results and constant feedback.

It would be the height of folly—to say nothing of patronizing arrogance—to say that these differences are without effect or affect. The actual import of these differences is arguable because the jury is still out. But, to argue that the effects can be ignored because there are more pressing things to worry about is foolish and ultimately self-defeating.

The demographic hole is becoming deeper in corporate training organizations. The greybeards in senior positions show little inclination to leave. (After all, what does retirement mean to an increasingly older workforce?) Meanwhile, the learner audience is bifurcating into older and younger groups with the middle group regularly thinned out by reductions in force, downsizing, acquisitions, outsourcing, and flat job creation. This phenomenon just drives a greater wedge of incomprehension into the landscape.

Or, as Frank Zappa sang in 1966, "There's no way to delay that trouble comin' every day."

Tails, You Win Again—Age Doesn't Matter.

Worrying about the age of learners is another way that some designers waste time. The research around GenX/Y/Z or whatever label you stick on them (keeping in mind that nobody asks them how they would identify themselves) pales in comparison to the body of research on adult learning in general. One variable that can safely be factored out of the equation is age. There's much more that unites the corporate workforce than divides it. The adult learning theory of Malcolm Knowles is as good a description of your average GenX/Y/Z as it is of a typical baby boomer (Knowles, Holton, & Swanson, 2005):

➤ *The need to know:* Adult learners need to know why they need to learn something before initiating the learning process.

➤ *Learner self-concept:* Adults need to be responsible for their own decisions and to be treated as capable of self-direction.

➤ *Role of learners' experience:* Adult learners have a variety of experiences of life that represent the richest resource for learning.

➤ *Readiness to learn:* Adults are ready to learn the things they need to know to cope effectively with life situations.

➤ *Orientation to learning:* Adults are motivated to learn to the extent that they perceive that it will help them perform tasks they confront in their life situations.

Instead of worrying about the generation gap, energy should be spent focusing on making the experience interesting and useful as learning in and of itself and designing an experience relevant to the person, not some abstract group.

Exploration is more engaging than recitation. Doing things with some measure of control is better than authoritarian lock-step. Telling people things they already know is less likely to keep them engaged than exposing them to new worlds. Giving them a reason they can identify with is more effective than saying "because I said so" as a rationale. Nothing new there and nothing that's got much of anything to do with whether I'm 18 or 48 years old.

What Does All This Mean in the Day-to-Day?

Now it's time for our mythic two-handed economist to get off the dime. How can learning professionals take the insights provided by their warring angels and turn them into action in the daily pursuit of their profession? Here's my take.

Awareness

Of course, there will still be a learning function. The nature of a volatile world simply demands it. People are too busy and not always ready to respond to change because they're not looking at the big picture when change strikes. Nevertheless, a centralized, walled-off group that only talks to itself, its peers, and industry soothsayers is setting itself up for trouble if not irrelevance.

Make the borders separating the compartments more porous. Spend some quality time with the members of your audience, get to know their view of the world, bring them into the planning process. Learning professionals are always asking for a seat at the table. Maybe it ought to work the other way. The learners should have a seat at the learning function's table. You never know what will pop up at a good lunchroom bull session!

Motivation

Motivation is paired with awareness. The more people see that they're involved in the process, the more engaged they're likely to be. The closer you are to the learner, the more likely you'll be delivering an experience that he or she immediately sees is valuable. You can also do a much better job of providing a communication loop that keeps learners aware of the value of what you're providing. Of course, if you're going to open up the communications and start actively touting your contribution as a learning professional, be sure that you make good on the claims.

Personalization

Again, both sides of the discussion are true. Rather, the truth lies somewhere in the middle. How do you find that optimal point? Making an audience analysis a mandatory part of any program design isn't a bad place to start. I did an analysis of the audience at a global investment bank and identified three distinct demographics, each with different backgrounds, motivations, and work environments—and that didn't take account of regional culture or language. Paying attention to these profiles made a world of difference in program design and delivery. Designing programs that allow learners to test out of the program, in whole or in part, is another strategy for solving the problem that also builds goodwill and increases efficiency—unless some version of the number of butts in seats is your metric, in which case you've got a problem going in.

It is not practical to treat all learners the same because experience and personal history make every person's starting point unique. However, creating a training program that focuses separately on each individual is impractical. The key to success is finding a balance between group and individual focus.

Theory

Theory is tied to the previous issue, personalization. Distinctions do matter, but they don't matter absolutely. Providing alternatives can help bridge any gaps related to age, experience, or education. Most important, awareness and understanding of both the audience and the needs of the organization in all their richness are critical—another balancing act that learning professionals have to master. There aren't any silver bullets, just a lot of hard work and careful thought.

Overcoming the Lies With Truth

Learners: You can't live with 'em, and you can't live without 'em. Yeah, I know, this statement is about as old as the koans (Yamada, 2004) discussed in a Philosophy 101 course or the jargon shoveled around boardrooms (Fugere, Hardaway, & Warshawsky, 2005), for example:

➤ The next sentence is true.
➤ The previous sentence is false.
➤ The sound of one hand clapping.
➤ Get used to it. Make it your friend.

Nevertheless, it should be clear that the underlying argument here in defense of the faith is the tension between perspectives emphasizing either the particular or the general views. Most learning professionals ply their craft within organizations, that is, collections of individuals engaged in group activities with the goal of promoting some collective good. At least, the hope is that it's for the good, the Enrons of the world notwithstanding.

Integrity and professional standards drive learning professionals to protect the individuality of each learner whenever possible. Demands of time and resources necessitate reliance upon LCDs for efficiency. These opposing perspectives and the decisions they necessitate shift continually, creating the music that learning professionals dance to daily.

Here's hoping this brief discussion has added some lyrics to that music.

The Lie	The Truth
Learners need the guidance of a top-down learning organization.	People are increasingly aware of their own career development and respond to market forces faster than an organization can.
Learners already know what they need to know; we just have to get out of the way.	The modern work environment is too complex and fast changing for an organization to trust solely in self-development.
People don't really care about learning, just results.	Presented with interesting and valuable possibilities, people enjoy the learning process itself.
Learners take it on trust that a learning event will be valuable experience.	In the age of broken social contracts dealing with employment, people need to be shown just why a learning event will be beneficial.
Learners are essentially the same.	Each individual has his or her own need for self-expression, validation, and career development.
Every learner is a unique individual.	Focusing on differences can paralyze an organization.
Younger learners are inherently different from older ones.	Human beings have much more in common than anything that might set them apart.
Age doesn't matter.	Learners under the age of 30 have grown up in a radically different world compared to their "elders." To ignore this fact is to set yourself up for trouble in reaching your audience.

References

Atherton, J.S. (2005). "Tacit Knowledge and Implicit Learning. *Learning and Teaching: L and T Template.* http://www.learningandteaching.info /learning/tacit.htm.

Catholic Encyclopedia (volume 1). (1907). "Advocatus Diaboli" and "Promotor Fidei." New York: Robert Appleton Company. Online edition: Knight, K. (2003). http://www.newadvent.org/cathen /index.html.

Christensen, M. (2005). "The New Social Contract." In *Learning Rants, Raves, and Reflections,* E. Masie (editor). San Francisco: Pfeiffer/John Wiley & Sons.

Fugere, B., C. Hardaway, and J. Warshawsky. (2005). *Why Business People Speak Like Idiots: A Bullfighter's Guide.* New York: Free Press.

Hirsch, E.D., J.F. Kett, and J. Trefil (editors). (2002). "The Devil Is in the Details." *The New Dictionary of Cultural Literacy: What Every American Needs to Know* (3rd edition). New York: Houghton Mifflin.

Knowles, M.S., III, E.F. Holton, and R.A. Swanson. (2005). *The Adult Learner: The Definitive Classic in Adult Education and Human Resource Development* (6th edition). Burlington, MA: Elsevier/Butterworth-Heinemann.

Thredgold, J. (2001). "The Economist's Joke Book." Salt Lake City: Thredgold Economic Associates. http://www.thredgold.com/html /joke.html.

Yamada, K. (2004). *Gateless Gate: The Classic Book of Zen Koans.* Somerville, MA: Wisdom Publications.

Zappa, F., and the Mothers of Invention. (1966). "Trouble Every Day." *Freak Out.* Verve/MGM.

Lies About the Design of Learning

Melinda Jackson

Is instructional design dead? That was the question posed to the small group of professionals gathered in a think-tank setting to talk about ways to improve organizational learning and human performance. Chief learning officers, human resources directors, training managers, e-learning vendors, and professional consultants sat closely in a semicircle, an intimate arrangement for exchanging professional advice and sharing lessons learned.

As soon as the question was asked, I began to rise from my seat for an impassioned reply defending instructional design (ID). "Um, uh, wait, what the...?" were the only words I could muster. I'd meant to issue a rallying cry, but I barely punctuated the mounting din of disapproval from the others: "Instructional design is irrelevant," "You really just need subject matter experts," "It may be good for front-end analysis, but it's otherwise unproductive," "ID simply takes too long and costs too much," "If you want boring learning, follow the ID models," "Instructional design is out of touch with the dynamics of business," and so forth.

I was dumbfounded and piqued. My dismay went beyond the dismissal of my profession. (Ouch, that did hurt actually!) My primary shock was in reaction to the dismissal of the discipline of design from learning.

Design is the human tradition of creative engineering. Design is everywhere and is in everything humans make and do. Design invents, crafts, creates, constructs, and forges. Design plans for successful outcomes aligned with intention. "Design" is both a verb and a noun; it is a process and a philosophy; it is about function and about form; it is about aesthetics and about usability.

Imagine architecture without design. Imagine fashion, theater, or fine arts without design. Imagine electrical or mechanical engineering without design, marketing and advertising without design, and new products or services commenced without design.

Now, imagine learning without design.

The underlying frustration I witnessed from the roomful of learning professionals was based on the bad reputation of workplace training. The bad rep is warranted because most instruction, whether classroom or computer-based, is bad. Consider the courses that involve three days of droning about policies and procedures at new employee orientation, a refresher course that is the same as last year's, a team building seminar delivered in lecture format, or an e-learning course that consists mostly of bulleted text, animations, and nothing that couldn't be learned in five minutes leafing through the employee handbook.

By debunking the lies about the design of learning, I hope to persuade you of the opportunities to rescue learning from its current abysmal state. By applying ID principles and processes to the learning domain, effective and *enjoyable* [pause inserted here for audience gasp] training can be developed.

Lie #1: Instructional Design Is Irrelevant.

Instructional design is relevant because its purpose is to make learning relevant. Perhaps this misconception originates from staid models of ID that still permeate popular notions of how learning design is practiced.

Anyone who has worked in ID in industry, academia, government, or military training and indoctrination in the past 20 years has experienced the arcane obedience demanded by practitioners of certain behaviorist-oriented system models. There is nothing inherently wrong in the models; they are quite informative and useful to learning design. The distaste for models comes from a strict adherence to a lengthy and linear development process that allows for no deviation from its rule set.

ID encompasses much more than following a model or rule set. In fact, ID models are best used as frameworks for design. As frameworks, these models can provide a flexible platform from which the designer can construct the most appropriate and effective learning experience. Strict interpretation of models results in a mechanical orientation to design. As a systems-thinking approach, learning design should be considered from an ecosystem mindset, an organic orientation to the many aspects of human cognition and experience.

ID models provide a framework of processes and procedures that allow the designer to attend to the functional components of instruction. These frameworks ensure that proper attention is given to every component within the instructional system, including goals, audience, subject matter, materials, and environment. From this holistic viewpoint, the system subcomponents guide the instructional designer into the important decisions necessary to accommodate learner attitudes and motivation, select strategies for retention and transfer, and guide the learners' achievement of instructional objectives.

Principles of design also attend to the balance of form and function. That is, good design combines usefulness with appeal.

Brenda Laurel (2003, p. 17) introduces design research as "a set of methods and practices aimed at getting insight into what would serve or delight people. It investigates behind the scenes, looking at individuals, situated contexts, cultures, forms, history, and even business models for clues that can inform design."

The many details of ID require a nuanced practitioner. Understanding the audience requires knowledge of their needs for training and their attitudes about the subject. Selecting the best instructional strategy for the subject matter requires understanding the context of application. Designers must draw on the culture, patterns of usage, and common practices of the targeted learners and workplace setting. Spot-on, effective, and engaging training is the result of reasoned and informed design process decisions.

Lie #2: All You Need Is a Subject Matter Expert (SME).

The implication behind the statement, "All you need is a SME" is that anyone can do ID. This fallacy probably arises from the close personal experience with instruction that is shared universally among humans. Everyone has received instruction and given instruction at some point in his or her life. Accumulated time in classrooms and training centers amounts to tens of thousands of hours. People are instructional power users, training superconsumers, but their familiarity with instruction leads to a leap in logic: "I know how to do this."

However, one must possess a specialized knowledge and skill set to produce good ID. It does not require an advanced degree. Like any other activity, study and practice improve performance, and the personal passion for a discipline advances competency. A devotion to a discipline means one tries and learns and tries again in quest of excellence. Insights of experience are gained that lead to decisions based in wisdom. This is how someone becomes competent at designing instructional materials and learning experiences.

Because learning is a natural human activity, some say that designing learning is natural, too. Good design is neither natural nor easy. Design is fraught with problems, constraints, and real-world dilemmas.

A good instructional designer is a multidisciplinary practitioner. Part teacher, psychologist, sociologist, anthropologist, and cultural epicure, instructional designers aim to change human knowledge, attitudes, and behaviors by engineering transformative learning experiences. To meet this challenge, designers must integrate a wide range of information references and design activities.

A blend of special knowledge and work experiences gives designers the intellectual foundation to wisely analyze and smartly craft learning

---

A blend of special knowledge and work experiences gives designers the intellectual foundation to wisely analyze and smartly craft learning experiences.

---

experiences. In the book *Blink,* Malcolm Gladwell (2005) provides fascinating case studies about the differences in thinking patterns among experts as compared to novice or even less practiced professionals. It seems expert knowledge naturally leads to intuition, or at least cultivates highly reliable instincts, that experts apply to decision making.

When I hear the claim, "All you really need is a SME," I nod my head in agreement and add "plus a good instructional designer." Indeed, I hope to have a good SME on every project. A SME's knowledge and experience of the target learners and subject matter area are invaluable to design. Nevertheless, that knowledge alone does not make for knowing how to construct effective, efficient, and engaging training. On the contrary, the SME may be so expert that he or she cannot relate to the needs of a novice or intermediary learner.

What are the basic skills you should seek in an instructional designer? A meta-analysis of ID studies by Kenny et al. (2005) compared a half-dozen quantitative (with statistically significant numbers represented) and qualitative studies about what instructional designers do. Not surprisingly, instructional designers do many things other than design: project management, training and supervision, meetings with clients, marketing and sales, presentations, and so forth. But the skill set was definitive. The skills applied most by instructional designers are

> ➤ communication skills
> ➤ knowledge of ID models
> ➤ problem-solving skills
> ➤ decision-making skills
> ➤ technology skills.

Not everyone is equally capable of analyzing human behavior, blending theories of cognitive science with practical knowledge of application, and examining the influence of popular culture. On top of all that, an instructional designer must also keep with the pulse of societal change, hone messages to essential elements for understanding, and select the materials and technologies that best support human learning and performance. These are the specialized skills and professional endeavors of instructional designers.

Lie #3: Instructional Design Is a Front-End-Only Process.

The myth that learning design is a front-end-only process is probably due to over-the-wall syndrome. "Over-the-wall" is common business vernacular for describing a project that is piecemeal; that is, parts of the project are created in isolation and then assembled at the implementation stage. Such an approach inevitably leads to poor results.

Good ID requires an organic, holistic approach. This approach involves consideration of the entire ecosystem in which learning occurs, and it includes the designer in the entirety of the project lifecycle.

Indeed, overseeing the front-end concept and design phase are primary duties of the instructional designer, but the instructional designer's input on production decisions and implementation strategies is invaluable. The instructional designer also evaluates the effectiveness of the training—both formative (during development) and summative (after implementation).

Although creating great training is a team sport, the instructional designer is a key strategic player on the team. The instructional designer has varying degrees of responsibility throughout project phases.

I like to consider a five-phase approach to training development and delivery:

1. concept and design
2. development and production
3. implementation
4. evaluation
5. sustainability.

Concept and Design

During the concept and design phase, the instructional designer plans a pedagogical approach that takes into account

➤ the business problem that the training is to address
➤ the knowledge, skills, and attitudes to be imparted by training
➤ curricular prerequisites
➤ learner characteristics
➤ motivational strategies
➤ content structures

➤ logistical issues
➤ requirements for the training environment.

The instructional designer also establishes curricular priorities by sorting through content for the most essential knowledge and skills. Not all knowledge is equal. I usually filter potential content into three categories:

➤ must know/do
➤ important to know/do
➤ nice to know/do.

Many instructional projects fail because essential learning is diluted by voluminous content. To counter this problem, some of the important to know/do and all of the nice to know/do content can be put into resources and references that accompany the training. Sometimes called criticality sorting, the process of choosing content coverage and weighing content importance is an essential task of the instructional designer.

> The instructional designer does not engineer project concept and design alone. It is important to include an entire team in creative generation; not only does creativity benefit from multiple insights and perspectives, but the whole team contributes and buys into the project design.

Development and Production

During the development and production phase, a detailed outline of the content and instructional strategies is handed off to multimedia writers and multimedia artists. Whether building computer-based training (CBT) or instructor-led training (ILT), a team of experienced writers and graphic designers works cooperatively to create the instructional assets. During this time, the instructional designer is mainly on call to handle questions, to review, and to ensure that instructional assets meet design specifications. Also during this phase, the instructional designer oversees usability testing and evaluates the instructional effectiveness of the new materials.

Implementation

The implementation phase often includes train-the-trainer or other directives for product use. The instructional designer frequently acts as the first trainer or facilitator of a new learning product in cooperation with the client or the program owner within the organization. The instructional designer engages knowledge transfer and assists with any unforeseen implementation issues that arise.

Evaluation

The evaluation phase is actually an iterative cycle that begins early in the design and production phases and then again after implementation. The instructional designer creates assessments for learning outcomes and for project evaluation. Short-term measures of learning gains and learner satisfaction are gathered easily through nominal assessment means. Long-term results, such as organizational impacts and return-on-investment (ROI), are considerably more difficult to measure and require collaboration between the instructional designer and the client to access both data and people to conduct additional assessments over time.

Sustainability

The sustainability phase is often an overlooked component of ID. It is a mistake not to consider how a learning project will be maintained and supported. Part of the role of the instructional designer is to consider updated needs and localization (translation into other languages and culture uses). Planning for sustainability is done during the overall design of the product but also occurs as additions or updates of content and translations of the product.

Lie #4: Instructional Design Takes Too Long and Costs Too Much.

The idea that ID takes too long and is way too resource-intensive is often attributable to scoping or project management. Project management gone awry leads to waste. Ill-conceived projects take too long and cost too much; this is true for any type of project.

Real-world evidence proves it is wasteful to *not* design. Ineffective training is a huge waste of organizational time and resources. Corporate workers and their managers yearn for training that makes a difference, training that improves job performance and productivity, and training that develops careers.

New tools and practices in ID aim to achieve better results quickly. Iterative development cycles, rapid prototyping, and early usability testing keep design targeted to delivering top-quality training in shortened timeframes. ID is an agile process that adapts to the constraints of the project.

Richard W. Pew, an authority on human factors and industrial design, said the design process "is the successive application of constraints until only a unique product is left" (Norman, 1988, p.158). Instructional designers make decisions based on the affordances and attributes of each project, including time and resource limits.

Lie #5: Instructional Design Makes Learning Tedious and Not Very Fun.

As for the notion that ID takes the fun out of learning, I can only assume this again stems from training's bad reputation. No-fun learning is contrary to the real purposes of ID.

Successful ID keeps the learner as the centerpiece of the design process. In Robert Gagne's nine-step model of instruction, engaging the learner's attention is step one (Gagne, Briggs, & Wager, 1988). Piquing learner interest and motivation is crucial to instructional success. Learner engagement is the critical factor to ensure learning outcomes. If you lose a learner's attention, you have lost the educational moment. Brenda Laurel (2003, p. 17) notes, "...design research betters the odds for a successful, even delightful, match between an audience's needs and desires with a product, service or experience."

Some notions about learning and fun are attributable to value differences—often spurred by cultural or generational differences. A former employer, who was an octogenarian and a first-generation American, told me, "Learning should be hard. If it doesn't hurt the head then you're not thinking hard enough!"

Today's learners crave learning experiences that are engaging, interesting, and entertaining. Although I think the word "edutainment" is a misnomer, and some call it an oxymoron, as a designer I strive to entertain the learner by inserting humor, interesting stories, and surprising elements into instruction. When I have a learner's attention, I have access to the learner's mind.

Lie #6: Instructional Design Is Out of Touch With the Dynamics of Business.

I hope debunking this lie, that ID is out of touch with the dynamics of business, is a foregone conclusion by now. The goals of business are to deliver the best products and services, to beat the competition, and to improve the profits of the organization. ID is a powerful ally to business goals.

The past two decades of worldwide industry have been marked by process-based initiatives that differentiate the lean manufacturer and win marketplace dominance. Business process improvements lead to greater efficiencies and effectiveness. These business initiatives arose from systems analysis and process models that seek to build agility, flexibility, and reliability into every function of business.

Similarly, ID is a process model that seeks agility, flexibility, and reliability. The ultimate goal of instruction is to influence and to improve human performance. For business, human capital and human performance are synonymous.

To grow and prosper, business must maintain a well-trained and ready workforce. Within the hypercompetitive global economy, fortunes are won or lost based on companies' ability to adapt to changing markets and consumer drivers. Change requires learning or relearning, or unlearning and learning anew.

Perhaps it is not ID that is out of touch with the dynamics of business, but rather business that is out of touch with the dynamics of learning.

My former employer, the octogenarian I mentioned before, was George Kozmetsky (Dr. K), a sage businessperson who founded Teledyne, served as dean of the University of Texas at Austin School of Business, and was the first chairman of the board at Dell, among many other distinctions. He frequently counseled aspiring entrepreneurs who sought his advice: "You can only grow your business as fast as you train your employees and your suppliers, your customers, and your customers' customers." From Dr. K's long experience in both business and education, he declared learning to be the heartbeat of the healthy enterprise.

Perhaps it is not ID that is out of touch with the dynamics of business, but rather business that is out of touch with the dynamics of learning. It is imperative that ID be seen as a strategic process for business. Until then, the lies about the design of learning will prevail, and mediocre training will remain the norm.

Instructional Design Checkpoints

Instructional design is both a creative and pragmatic endeavor. A mixed repertoire of process models, cognitive theories, and instructional strategies comprise every designer's toolkit. Although the instructional designer must adapt these tools to each project's unique requirements, there is a set of universal checkpoints to use along the way to help structure content, accommodate the learner, and work with a design team.

Each of these checkpoints is described in more detail in the following sections.

Structuring Content
- Focus squarely on the problem to be solved.
- Write measurable (actionable) performance objectives.
- Prioritize and structure content. Filter must-know/do from important-to-know/do knowledge and skills.
- Identify common mistakes and misconceptions that can interfere with performance. Uncovering such misconceptions advances real understanding.
- Design instructional experiences that include relevant examples, explanations, analogies, and stories to keep learners

engaged and content interesting; include drama and humor where appropriate.

➤ Choose instructional strategies germane to content.

➤ Provide practice opportunities (interactivity). Learning by doing builds understanding more effectively than learning by watching, listening, or reading.

➤ Provide meaningful feedback to instructional activities. Feedback is a teaching moment, not a confirmation of right or wrong.

➤ Create assessments clearly tied to the content and expected outcomes. Include knowledge checks during instruction along with formal assessment at the end.

Accommodating the Learner Audience

➤ Understand your audience. Identify learners' interests and motivation. The instruction must be able to answer the question: "What's in it for me?" for learners within the first few minutes of instruction.

➤ Provide learners with strategies for retention and ideas about how to transfer new knowledge and skills to their jobs.

➤ Conduct usability tests and ensure that training materials align with learners' needs.

➤ Include job aids or other resources as take-away materials to help learners apply new knowledge.

➤ Plan for how learning will be followed up on the job and reinforced later through updates, refreshers, or advanced training.

Working With a Design Team

➤ Include the entire team in the creative concept, design, and planning for the project.

➤ Identify project constraints together (time, money, special circumstances, and so forth).

➤ Design with sustainability in mind to ensure that content can be updated or translated.

➤ Work closely with writers and multimedia artists during development and production of instructional assets to ensure instructional integrity.

➤ Prepare and provide knowledge transfer to end client or project owner, and assist with implementation.

➤ Evaluate project effectiveness and disseminate lessons learned back to the team.

Overcoming the Lies With Truth

Instructional design is under attack as an ineffective and inefficient practice that produces lackluster results. The truth is that reasoned and balanced instructional design produces effective, efficient, and satisfying results.

There is a maxim in business: "Bad workers always blame their tools." ID tools and processes are not at fault, but their application has been faulty. Applying process models, cognitive theories, and instructional strategies to inform decisions, instructional design requires agility and adaptability to the unique constraints of each project. The experienced ID practitioner brings the toolset and the proper skill set to designing the right experience for the right learners in the right context with the right content supported by the right motivational and engagement strategies to support the right learning outcomes.

The Lie	The Truth
Instructional design is irrelevant.	The purpose of instructional design is to make learning relevant. Instructional design models provide flexible platforms for designing the best and most appropriate learning experience.
All you need is a SME.	Every project requires not only a good SME but also a good instructional designer. Not everyone can do ID; one must possess a specialized knowledge and a honed skill set to produce good instructional design.
Instructional design is a front-end-only process.	As an organic, holistic approach, ID considers the entire eco-system in which learning occurs. By involving the instructional designer throughout the project, cohesiveness of the phases and overall quality are ensured throughout. Designers act as quality assurance for the entirety of the project lifecycle.
Instructional design takes too long and costs too much.	It is wasteful *not* to design. ID tools and practices such as iterative development cycles, rapid prototyping, and early usability testing keep design targeted at achieving better results quickly. ID can adapt to the constraints of the project.
Instructional design makes learning tedious and not very fun.	Learner experience is the centerpiece of the ID process. Designers make learning interesting by inserting humor, compelling examples, stories, and surprising elements into instruction.
Instructional design is out of touch with the dynamics of business.	ID is an ally to business goals. The ultimate goal of instruction is to influence and improve human performance. Like any business process improvement model, ID should be applied with agility, flexibility, reliability, and effectiveness.

References

Gagne, R.M., L.J. Briggs, and W.W. Wager. (1988). *Principles of Instructional Design* (3rd edition). New York: Holt, Rinehart & Winston.

Gladwell, M. (2005). *Blink: The Power of Thinking Without Thinking.* New York: Little, Brown and Company.

Kenny, R.F., Z. Zhang, R.A. Schwier, and K. Campbell. (2005). "A Review of What Instructional Designers Do: Questions Answered and Questions Not Asked. *Canadian Journal of Learning and Technology, 31*(1), 9–26.

Laurel, B. (2003). *Design Research: Methods and Perspectives.* Cambridge, MA: MIT Press.

Norman, D.A. (1988). *The Design of Everyday Things.* New York: Doubleday.

Other Recommended Reading

Brown, J. (2002). *The Social Life of Information.* Boston: Harvard Business School Press.

Dick, W., and L. Carey. (1996). *The Systematic Design of Instruction* (4th edition). New York: HarperCollins.

Reigeluth, C. (editor). (1999). *Instructional-Design Theories and Models: A New Paradigm of Instructional Theory,* volume 2. Mahwah, NJ: Lawrence Erlbaum Associates.

Rosenberg, M. (2006). *Beyond E-Learning: Approaches and Technologies to Enhance Organizational Knowledge, Learning, and Performance.* San Francisco: Jossey-Bass.

Wiggins, G., and J. McTighe. (1998). *Understanding by Design.* Alexandria, VA: Association for Supervision and Curriculum Development.

Lies About
Careers in Learning

Beth Thomas

What are the lies about careers in learning? I've talked to several people about their careers in learning. Some say they are at a standstill, others indicate that they are being categorized into either instructor-led training or e-learning, some report that training managers have no control and that training is not a strategic driver in companies. But, other learning professionals are saying it's the best time ever to be in the field of training and development. What do you believe? I've heard it all and am going to analyze some lies that have surfaced regarding careers in the learning industry.

Not too long ago, I was at an interview with the president of a *Fortune* 500 company. I was contemplating leaving a great career to join the company; we'll call this company Scenic. I was coming from a company where learning was valued and I was at the table. However, it had taken a long time to get there, and I wasn't sure I wanted to give up my seat at the table quite yet. One of the first questions I asked the president was, "Is learning at the table at Scenic?" His answer was interesting. He said "No, which is why we want to bring you on board." My next question was, "What difference would it make if I were on board?" He replied, "You could help teach us why you should be at the table."

I loved his humility and honesty. He knew in his heart that learning was important to the growth of the company and to employee development, but, clearly, Scenic was struggling with the same thing many companies do. They wanted learning to be at the table, but there wasn't a champion telling them why or how.

Some just have the wrong idea about training. It's overhead, or it's a staff role so it's not important. Still, it's a department they've always had. Why is that? Why do companies have training departments if they don't want to fully utilize the benefits they can bring to the company?

My story has a happy ending. I joined Scenic, and soon after I was at the table. At a senior management meeting six months after I started with the company, the president announced that the number-one business initiative for the year was training. And as a follow-up comment, the president actually pointed to me sitting in a crowd of hundreds and said "I am looking to Beth Thomas to help get us where we need to be." To have such executive support is euphoric for training managers, but it doesn't come easy. Senior managers and leaders of companies are expected to support training, to do the right thing, and to go along with all the magazine articles and books stating that training and learning should always be on the forefront of a company's business strategy or at the very least aligned with the business.

Very few training managers spend their time educating the senior managers on the value learning has to a company in business terms. Actually, they don't believe they can make a difference, and they are afraid to ask to be at the table. They are more comfortable staying under the radar. They don't think it's a war worth fighting. This is not a comfortable situation; hence the first lie about careers in learning.

Lie #1: Training Managers Can't Make It to the Table.

Training managers can make a difference and dine with the executives! Senior managers do expect you to come to them and challenge them on how learning can be at the table and add value to a business. If you are waiting for an invitation to do this, your career may be over by the time you receive one.

To get invited to sit at the table, training managers first need to learn the business. Without this knowledge, senior managers won't have the confidence that you and the training department are aligned with the business. You have to know the business to understand how to help the business.

Do you understand what it means to be aligned with your business? For training managers, it means integrating yourself into the business and understanding the top challenges or the pain of the business at all times. If an outsider asked your chief executive officer to list the top three challenges of your business and then asked you the same question, would you both answer the same way? You should. That is how closely aligned you should be with your business. Know what makes it tick, be aware of what the strategy is, where the pain is, and where opportunity lies. You have to be flexible and dynamic to support the business when it changes—which nowadays happens frequently!

To be in sync with the business, you have to work on the few critical initiatives your company is executing this year. You have to be visible to the leadership team. You have to have an executive sponsor. Most of all, you have to prove yourself, create small wins for the business, and communicate them, early and often. Market yourself and your team, but make sure your marketing is always attached to the business problem you solved. And, always be part of the solution!

As a training manager, your most important role is being the voice and face of the training team. It's about more than educating, it's about getting results. Before, the measurements of training success were about how many people you trained, how many classes you offered, and how people felt about them. Now what you really have to do is show how the training has increased sales, reduced costly errors, decreased turnover, or made employees more effective and productive. Training can be the single most important contributor to the success of costly projects, such as business process changes, mergers and acquisitions, and major system implementations. Without you, these costly projects will fail. If you take note of the aforementioned statistics and communicate them to senior managers who focus on that information during business challenges, you will never have a problem getting a seat at the table!

As a training manager, your most important role is being the voice and face of the training team. It's about more than educating, it's about getting results.

Lie #2: Once You Are in Training, You'll Always Be in Training.

Whether you are an instructional designer, trainer, e-learning developer, or training manager, there are endless opportunities available to you. Whether you have been in training for two years or 20, the experience you have gained being in training can open up doors to a multitude of other careers. Training professionals who are passionate about training and possess a high degree of emotional intelligence are able to build relationships at all levels and understand people and how they react to change. This experience is invaluable for many different careers.

In addition, the mix of technology and instructional design is also a great skill to have. If you have both, you are an incredible asset to many different companies and careers. If you have technical skills, there are all types of careers in web and graphic design; you could even work for a technology training vendor or as a consultant.

If you are a trainer or facilitator, the presentation skills that you have and the ability to engage with an audience and build relationships quickly are all competencies needed in a variety of jobs. If you wanted to branch out, there are several options available to you. For example, you could work with your favorite technology training vendor in sales or as an integration or implementation partner. There is so much that you can bring to that type of company. What about web or graphic design for e-learning developers? What about starting your own company and being an independent consultant?

If you are good at what you do, there are endless opportunities to help struggling companies bring training to the forefront as a strong component to their business strategies. What about going into a line position with a business? With the knowledge you acquire as a trainer or developer, you already know the business well enough to branch out into line positions with the departments you support. With the competencies you have within training, you can break into almost any career.

What helps you discover your new career using your competencies is creating a perfect job scenario. Have you ever done this? It is a great exercise to help you find the job of your life! I did this once and documented first what type of work makes me happy and what types of work I am passionate about and then presented the information to my president. Guess what? The position was created, and I got my dream job! Remember, sometimes you get what you ask for. It's all about creating a job and then finding it. What are *you* waiting for? Create your perfect job scenario and go find it!

The bottom line is the competencies you have built during a career in training have created many opportunities that are yours when you want them. However, you have to work at it. Remember, networking is critical to any career change. It is critically important to keep in touch with your contacts in all lines of business; there will be a time when you need them. When you are ready for a change, don't be afraid to reach out to your contacts and tell them you are looking for something new. Get on those websites and post your résumé. Sign up for executive search services, which provide great advice and have access to many different jobs. Get the help you need to prepare for a successful career change. Don't sit back and wait for someone to come to you. Take charge of your destiny, seize control of your career, and be happy!

Lie #3: It's Hard to Move Up in Training Without a Training-Related or Advanced Degree.

Baloney! Some of the best training executives that I have met do not have any formal education in training. How many times have you heard someone say they their best learning experiences were in a classroom or during an online event? Probably no one! How much of being a good training leader or training professional is about the formal education you have received? Most have learned from their life experiences. They have gone to the college of life where the experiential learning has given them the capabilities to be incredible training leaders.

Many training executives come from operational backgrounds or from other areas of the business, making them even more valuable because they understand business and not just training. They also have a great sense and understanding of what people need and how to meet their needs quickly and effectively. They understand technology, when to use it, and when not to. They understand the importance of building relationships at all levels within the organization and the value of getting an executive sponsor who can help them get the visibility they need to be at the table. They also understand how to get results and how *not* to get caught up in theory. They understand how to best utilize their people, their colleagues, and their peers as champions to generate speed in an area where it is critical to success. They understand the importance of proving their value every day! These are things successful training leaders do every day, not in the classroom, but in their jobs. These actions will continue to help escalate the training leader's career. The real point is that these items are taught more in the working world through experience than in a college classroom.

In 1999, I was previewed in *FASTCOMPANY* magazine as the "Queen of Training." I received more than 600 emails from interested readers and training colleagues from around the world. I responded to *each* email because I felt so honored that the readers thought I was doing something special. The most frequent question asked of me was, "How did you get where you are (assuming that was a good place)?" Most followed up with a question regarding my educational background that I had and whether I would advise them to get a degree in training or organization development or even an advanced degree. I replied to each one, "What you need is passion for your work and what you do every day."

Some wise person has been quoted as saying that if you find a job you love, you'll never work a day in your life. Passion for your work will get you further than any advanced degree. Passion helps you be really good at what you do. People can see and sense your passion, and they derive energy from it. Having passion for my work has certainly paid off for me and for many of my most successful colleagues in the learning field.

I am certainly not stating that having an advanced degree or a degree in a training-related field is worthless. Such degrees have helped many people, but they are not necessary for moving ahead and getting the job of your dreams. Be passionate about what you do, believe in what you do, and your attitude can help you to get the position you have always dreamed about!

> If you have a desire to do what you're doing—if you're actually excited about it—that energy will stand out. You will be noticed by co-workers and executives alike. Driving passion is a great catalyst for getting your seat at the table.

Lie #4: Just Doing a Good Job is Good Enough.

Do you think it is a good thing to stay under the radar, to just keep your head down and work? Well, if the company needs to lay off folks and you have this attitude, you may be the first one to go! We live in a dog-eat-dog world where every day and every minute matter. You are only as good as you are today. You have to prove yourself repeatedly.

You have the opportunity to reinvent the work you do and also how you are seen in the organization. You have the opportunity to be seen as a hero or as worthless. Don't let prior mistakes take hold of you and crush your opportunity to rebound. It's easy to get caught in that mental game. You can always rebound, but do it quickly. Don't waste any time. Believe in yourself. To be seen as a high-potential employee, you must separate yourself as the creative one, the speedy one, or the one with the great attitude who always forges ahead and pushes the envelope. How do you compare to the industry's best practices in the way you have implemented learning in your organization or, even better, solved business problems with learning in your organization? Are you the one taking direction or giving the direction? Are you the one in the meeting who has little input or most of the input? Do you do your homework on how to make things better? Are you constantly challenging the status quo? If not, you should be.

I remember a few stories from my years in corporate life. One was a situation in which training wasn't core to the business, and I wanted to see how the organization could create a training department that was seen as adding business value. I did my homework to understand what the best training departments offered their corporations, and I shamelessly stole their models to implement within my own company. It took planning, it took work, and it took faith.

You need to engage an executive sponsor to help bring to the table some of the new ideas about the way things should be done. You need to be prepared with information about what you will provide, how you will provide it, where you will provide it, when you will provide it, who will provide it, and how you will measure it. I created a business plan, which included a 24-month plan, on how it would work; it was approved by the leadership team. That was the beginning of my rise within that company.

In another example, a company was involved in a merger, so, of course, downsizing was being discussed. Some of my friends and colleagues worked there, but they always tried to fly under the radar. The company's executives didn't even know who my colleagues were or what they did to contribute to the business. Needless to say, their low profiles likely hastened their departure from the company.

Remember that every day is a new day—make it what you want and you will reap the benefits.

Lie #5: Training Professionals Don't Get Any Respect.

Sometimes executives question the value that training brings to their company, and the training professionals really struggle to give them the information they need. One of the most important goals of training professionals should be to understand the business they are in and how they can best support it. When you do this, you will get the respect you deserve. You need to not only understand the business but also align your training goals and strategy with the business.

So many training managers get engrossed in the day-to-day management or their tactical solutions that they lose the vision and the importance of the big picture. They must continually align themselves and their training with the businesses they support and the executives who lead them.

Building relationships with your business executives is critical to gaining their respect, both as a professional and also as a leader of the training organization. You must validate and continually prove your worth to the organization. You are the face and the voice of the training department. If you stay aligned and work day in and day out with executives, you will gain the respect of the company and the leadership team. Once you understand the business, you will understand what it takes to show that training can and will add value to it.

A great way to do this is by getting involved in business-critical projects and creating solutions for key initiatives and business problems. Give business leaders the solutions they need, not necessarily the ones they ask for. Flex your muscles and show them that you know what you are talking about by thinking creatively and offering innovative solutions to their business problems. Give them solutions they never would have thought of without you. Understand your competition and how training has added value to their businesses.

Keep up-to-date on the challenges being currently faced by your business. Discuss these with the executives so that they see that you know not only what is happening in your own business but also what the competitors are doing. Continually market the wins that you have or, better yet, have your participants market your success for you. Their words will carry more weight in the organization. By doing these things, your job will be secure if downsizing ever looms over your business.

Lie #6: Careers in E-Learning Are the Only Learning Careers of the Future.

This lie is about as funny or as ridiculous as the assertion that appeared when e-learning first came out that instructor-led training would go away. Employees feared that their jobs were in jeopardy because they were classroom developers or trainers who didn't know anything about online training. The employees who were worried were often the ones who had received the best performance ratings and the largest bonuses based on their value to the organization. Learning professionals who design instructor-led classes will always be needed and are just as valuable as e-learning developers. Will instructor-led training evolve and change? I certainly hope so, but it will always be a key component of any training strategy.

Online learning has come a long way, but there remains plenty of opportunity in this area, which challenges and excites e-learning developers. Learning professionals must become better at figuring out how to deploy e-learning on multiple platforms, in bite-sized chunks, and with plenty of engagement and interactivity. At the same time, instructor-led training developers have an equal challenge. They must become more effective at designing training that is relevant, prescriptive, and available just in time. Both types of developers should challenge themselves in the field of informal learning and what that approach means to their business clients.

I hold trainers and facilitators in the highest regard simply because high-quality delivery resources are hard to find. Certainly there are plenty of people who deliver training for a living, but few are truly competent. I am not trying to be mean; I am being honest. I attend training conferences and see many presentations. Half the time, I want to poke my eyes out because I am so bored. In fairness, it's not easy to be an engaging subject matter expert and continually adjust to the needs of the audience. No one ever said training was easy. If you are one of the rare training professionals who can captivate an audience while they learn, then my hat goes off to you. You are one of the few who can name your price!

Developers and trainers face challenges also. For example, what about the use of gaming in the classroom? And, what about the use of Wikis, a piece of server software that allows users to freely create and edit web page content using any web browser? How about using blogs as part of an instructional strategy? Just think of the ways these new tools can be used to make training valuable to participants. New technologies and approaches give learning professionals the ability to understand their customers' expectations and challenges before they come to class, making it possible to exceed those expectations every time.

With all these challenges, training professionals have an enormous amount of work to do. They must learn to challenge themselves to think beyond the standard set of processes, methodologies, and tools they use to do their work to develop new, more creative ways to meet customers' needs.

This is the best time to have a career in learning. Are you up for the challenge to change the landscape of learning? Are you ready to be the best and to be a pioneer of new ideas, theories, and practices? Now's your chance to make your mark at training conferences and in the body of literature challenging the status quo.

Overcoming the Lies With Truth

Training managers are more than welcome to the business table once they've earned their seat there. Understand the business you work for and what you can do to support its critical few initiatives. Show the business staff you are an asset and a forerunner in learning by being a visible member of the leadership team. Engage executive sponsors in training initiatives by using business-speak to communicate, not training jargon. Communicate to them how training helped drive sales in the business and reduced costly mistakes, not how many people you've trained or how much they enjoyed your programs. Increasing financial success within your business will more than grab their attention. Keep in mind that business is dynamic so you must be, too.

Focusing on experimental learning will keep your business on the cutting edge and make you appear to be an agile learning professional. Use your agility to address the customer's needs. Keeping customers happy is a primary way to advance your career within the business. Get to know people at all levels of your business and find ways to optimize their work. This can make jobs flow smoother, quicker, and cheaper—a great combination to draw attention from executives.

Execute your learning initiatives and get results quickly! Communicate and market your wins and explain how they helped the business as a way of demonstrating that you have the business's needs in mind. Gaining a good reputation in your business can help you get invaluable contacts and footholds with similar corporations if you ever desire a change on your career path. If you are seeking change, you will be well equipped because competencies within the training field can be applied successfully in many fields. Table 4-1 has some ideas to get you started if you are contemplating a change.

Table 4-1. Some career search resources.

Job Listing Websites	Executive Search Websites
www.monster.com	www.netshare.com
www.careerbuilder.com	www.careerchange.com
www.6figurejobs.com	www.reactionsearch.com
www.snagajob.com	www.theladders.com
www.job.com	www.execunet.com
www.employmentguide.com	www.lucasgroup.com
www.ihirejobnetwork.com	www.hoovers.com
	www.therecruiternetwork.com

Always be on top of your game. Daily, you have the opportunity to be a hero or worthless—it's your choice. Keep in mind that the boss might be watching. A great way to stay on top of your training game is to know your competition's approach to training. Steal shamelessly to stay on the leading edge of training. Contributing new ideas within your business will make you an invaluable resource.

E-learning will not replace classroom-based learning. If you are good at what you do, no technology will outmode you. Stay on top of your game, communicate positively with executives, learn your business, and apply your knowledge to your work. Person-to-person contact will never be out of style, so if you can captivate a room, a seat at the business table is yours for the taking. Once you get there, if you keep challenging the way your business approaches learning, you'll have that seat as long as you're with the company, too.

The Lie	The Truth
Training managers can't make it to the table.	Training managers can make a difference and dine with the executives! Senior managers do expect you to come to them and challenge them on how learning can be at the table and add value to a business.
Once you are in training, you'll always be in training.	Training professionals who are passionate about training and possess a high degree of emotional intelligence are able to build relationships at all levels and understand people and how they react to change. This experience is invaluable for many different careers.
It's hard to move up in training without a training-related or advanced degree.	Some of the best training executives do not have any formal education in training. Experiential learning has given them the capabilities to be incredible training leaders. Passion for your work can get you further than any advanced degree.
Just doing a good job is good enough.	To be seen as a high-potential employee, you must separate yourself as the creative one, the speedy one, or the one with the great attitude who always forges ahead and pushes the envelope.
Training professionals don't get any respect.	One of the most important goals of training professionals should be to understand the business they are in and how they can best support it. When you do this, you will get the respect you deserve. You not only need to understand the business, but also you must align your training goals and strategy with the business.
Careers in e-learning are the only learning careers of the future.	Training professionals have an enormous amount of work to do in terms of instructor-led and online learning. They must learn to challenge themselves to think beyond the standard set of processes, methodologies, and tools they use to do their work to develop new, more creative ways to meet customers' needs.

Lies About Chief Learning Officers

Len Sherman

Over the past three years, I've gone from launching a large-scale learning outsourcing company to managing a global procurement services business to teaching business strategy at a Boston-based university. What this experience has taught me—other than that I'm still trying to figure out what I want to do when I grow up—is that the world looks very different, depending on which side of the desk you're sitting.

In the first of these endeavors, when I was promoting learning outsourcing, it was of paramount importance to make the case that chief learning officers (CLOs) needed a truly strategic partner to help rapidly upgrade the capabilities of their learning organizations. It was a tricky proposition to make because success depended on finding a visionary, action-oriented executive who, despite such leadership, lacked confidence in the capabilities of his or her own organization. Of course, when I found it wasn't always easy to sell large-scale outsourcing, it was convenient to conclude that the real problem was the absence of inspired leadership within the ranks of CLOs. After all, any real CLO would see that my services were the key to learning nirvana—or so I thought.

When I assumed profit-and-loss (P&L) responsibility for my next business endeavor, it quickly became apparent that as important as learning is, it was no longer the focal point of my business existence.

There were suddenly many value drivers competing for my time, and learning had to take its rightful place as only one of the concerns to address on my stretched schedule. Like many executives, I found that the squeaky wheel gets the grease, and unless my learning executive could make an effective case for more budget and organizational commitment, it was very easy to allow other urgent matters to fully absorb my energies. I learned that as much as most learning executives truly believe in the value of their profession, it would be a mistake to assume that all chief executive officers (CEOs) get it—all the more reason that CLOs need outstanding leadership skills to champion effective learning outcomes within their organizations.

When I joined the front lines of learning practitioners, as a professor in a master's of business administration program, I finally learned that doing learning rather than enabling the activity are two very different things. There are certainly myriad theories about where technology-based or classroom education is most important, but actually experiencing the learning process and observing the outcomes firsthand provided a much richer perspective than the management reports that I had reviewed in years past.

All of this got me thinking about what it takes to be an effective CLO in the current business environment—manager, leader, practitioner, or all of the above. There certainly have been a number of opinions expressed on this subject, with more than a fair share of misconceptions. To wade into this debate, this chapter summarizes what I consider to be the six most notable lies about CLOs.

Lie #1: CLOs Have a Seat at the Management Table.

One large misconception about the emergence of CLOs over the last two decades is that some think this has given the learning function considerable stature. As a result, people who believe this fall into another fallacy: CLOs have a seat at most organizations' management tables.

The title of chief connotes stature and authority. As an increasing number of companies and nonprofit institutions began to set up corporate universities and anoint new CLO positions through the 1980s and 1990s, it was natural to believe that the learning function had come into its own. In those heady days, many believed that

CLOs had finally earned the respect they so clearly deserved and could take their rightful place at the senior management table within their organizations.

Was the declaration of victory premature for CLOs? In 2002, I delivered a keynote address at *CLO Magazine's* first annual corporate education symposium entitled, "Chief Learning Officers: Where Do We Go From Here?" At the time, I presented a number of observations, anecdotes, and the results of a survey of the audience itself to suggest that many CLOs and other senior learning professionals perceived themselves to be more like Rodney Dangerfield ("I don't get no respect") than rising stars within their organizations.

Despite their low base of professional esteem, I asserted that CLOs had the need and opportunity to drive quantum improvements in the effectiveness of corporate education. I continued to say that those up to the challenge could not only create enormous value for their companies but also would demonstrate the caliber of leadership that had, in the past, propelled successful practitioners in other corporate functions to the CEO suite in the past. Why was this not true for the CLOs I queried?

The more ominous flip side to this call to arms, of course, was my caution that those who failed to realize the CLO's value creation imperative were unlikely to improve their professional esteem or enjoy the comforts of prolonged job security. Indeed, there have been numerous instances of involuntary CLO turnover, not to mention the closure of several corporate universities in the past few years to bear out this concern.

Based on my ongoing dialog with corporate learning practitioners and reviews of more recent survey results (Chief Learning Officer Business Intelligence Board, 2005), it is clear that CLOs have yet to achieve the impact or the stature that their title connotes. Largely, CLOs still think their profession is not widely respected or supported by business leaders, and they believe the profession is not delivering outstanding business outcomes for their organizations, as shown by the survey findings:

> ➤ Only 21 percent of surveyed learning practitioners perceive that senior management shares their belief that learning and

development are critically important to the success of their organization.

➤ A minority of respondents strongly agree that learning makes their organization a great place to work, allows for smooth promotion of employees, or contributes to employee retention.

➤ Only 21 percent report very high alignment between learning and development initiatives and specific competencies needed to achieve organizational success.

➤ Although 99 percent of organizations use performance reviews, only 38 percent report that performance reviews significantly influence learning and development.

Although spending levels on training are reported to be rising since hitting a nadir in the wake of 9/11, there are still big gaps in the extent of CLOs' oversight of corporate education activities across the extended enterprise. Technology-driven applications continue to grow, but successful deployments of simulations and other high impact e-learning interventions are still more aspirational than realized in most organizations.

In short, this view of the impact of CLOs and the state of corporate education is what the French might summarize thus: *"Plus ça change, plus c'est la meme chose"* ("The more things change, the more things remain the same"). This prevailing view suggests that the overarching lie about CLOs is that the learning function has finally gained considerable stature by earning a seat at the management table in most organizations. In fact, the evidence suggests that the CLO function is not currently performing anywhere near its potential and will not do so, absent a more radical change agenda driven by a new breed of CLO.

Lie #2: Executives Don't Understand the Value of Effective Corporate Training.

What makes these statistics on the seeming ambivalence to the importance of the CLO function so striking is their jarring disconnect with the business reality in most organizations. How can corporate education not be critically important in a world where we are well along in the transition to a knowledge-based economy?

Peter Drucker (2002, p. 124) noted that "the only way an organization in a knowledge-based economy and society can excel is through getting more out of the same kind of people;—that is, through managing its knowledge workers for greater productivity. It is, to repeat an old saying, 'to make ordinary people do extraordinary things.'" Drucker (1978, p. 290) also noted that "the most important, and indeed the truly unique, contribution of management in the 20th century was the 50-fold increase in the productivity of the manual worker in manufacturing" and that "to make knowledge work more productive will be the great management task of this century." From a corporate education standpoint, developing the skills necessary to excel in a knowledge-based economy is far more difficult and complex than developing the skills that were necessary to compete effectively in the industrial economy. One only needs to consider why customer service is often so poor to recognize the challenge and opportunity of excelling in a knowledge-based economy.

The need to renew workforce skills continually is accelerating in most industries. The time to market in many industries has shrunk by as much as 50 percent in the last five years. What that means is engineers need to develop faster, manufacturing needs to tool up faster, salesforces need to learn new product specs faster, and customer support needs to fix problems faster.

Skilled labor represents nearly 85 percent of all jobs in 2005, up from only 20 percent in 1950. The transition from an industrial to a knowledge economy has meant that more workers need to learn more skills than ever before, and the skills they need are not static. Some studies have estimated that half of all employee skills become outdated within three to five years.

All of these elements suggest that the business environment is getting tougher to operate in because demands on the workforces are increasing. The realities of operating in this competitive environment confront senior business executives every day. Therefore, it seems unlikely that the very executives who have demonstrated the vision and leadership to rise to the top of their organizations are somehow uniquely blind to the importance of workforce effectiveness. For CLOs, this raises the specter that the real issue here is dissatisfaction with the perceived impact of corporate learning initiatives and not a failure to appreciate the importance of workforce performance.

Indeed, available evidence confirms that most senior executives do recognize the importance of workforce effectiveness to business performance. Each year, Accenture Learning undertakes a global survey of approximately 200 C-level executives of *Fortune* Global 500 corporations on issues related to high-performing workforces. One of the striking findings from Accenture's 2003 study was that only about one-fourth of the senior executives polled believed that a considerable majority of their workforces had the skills necessary to execute their jobs at industry-leading performance levels. Furthermore, less than 10 percent of CEOs were satisfied with the skills of their critical workforces (figure 5-1). Note that far fewer CEOs were satisfied with current workforce performance levels than heads of human resources (HR). Not surprisingly, this same survey found that 75 percent of the executives polled indicated that people issues were more important in the current year than in the previous one.

Figure 5-1. Importance of workplace performance.

Percentage of business executives who agree that a considerable majority[1] of employees have the necessary skills to execute their jobs at industry-leading performance levels:

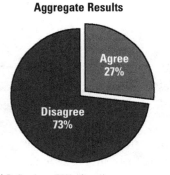

Aggregate Results

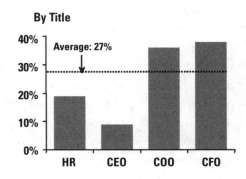

By Title

[1] Defined as >75% of employees

HR = human resources
CEO = chief executive officer
COO = chief operating officer
CFO = chief financial officer

Source: Accenture. (2003, January). *The High Performance Workforce Study.*

So the problem isn't that senior executives don't recognize the importance of workforce effectiveness. Rather the problem is that executives are not satisfied with the record of corporate learning in improving workforce performance. The cited Accenture survey found that only 12 percent of C-level executives were very satisfied with the performance of their corporate education organization.

Herein lay the great challenge and opportunity for corporate educators. Workforce performance is perceived as a critical strategic need by CEOs in most corporations. So, learning organizations have a tremendous opportunity to assume more leadership in deploying innovative, impacting, and relevant workforce improvement programs. The implicit threat of this course is that absent much needed improvements, learning groups may continue to be perceived as part of the problem, not the solution.

Lie #3: A CLO's Role Is as Important as Any Other Corporate Function.

I've been conducting my own anecdotal research regarding the effect of "Rodney Dangerfield syndrome" on corporate education departments. I've been asking many of my professional acquaintances in a variety of senior executive positions about their stereotypical impressions of various corporate functions like finance, legal, information technology (IT), HR, and learning. My intent has not been to assess any particular individual or department but to elicit general opinions on the professions themselves.

It's fair to say that there is often a healthy tension between P&L business unit leadership and all corporate staff functions, but corporate education is generally singularly held in lower regard than the other staff functions. When I've probed for the reasons, the common reaction has been that the training department doesn't add much value to the corporate enterprise. A variation on this theme is the self-reinforcing behavior of many business executives who acknowledged that they insist on retaining control of the "important" training functions, for example, sales, research and development, Six Sigma, and so forth, within their own functional or line organizations rather than handing off control to corporate training.

As further evidence, in 2003, the *Wall Street Journal* ran a story entitled "Learning Gurus Adapt to Escape Corporate Axes" (Pringle, 2003). Pringle explained that because of "a corporate phenomenon in the late 1990s...chief learning officers, popped up at companies like Pfizer, Coca Cola, Monsanto, and BT. Some of them installed new computer systems to help them pursue what was dubbed 'knowledge management.' Then came the collapsing stock market, corporate belt tightening and a backlash against technology, all of which prompted many companies to scrap knowledge-management [and learning] posts."

To add fuel to the fire, at about the same time, the trade journal *Workforce Management* published an article under the headline "For Some Chief Learning Officers, One of the Goals is Job Insecurity" (Gale, 2003). Gale noted, "John Coné retired as Dell's chief learning officer in August of 2001, but the company never replaced him. It wasn't because the CLO position is a passing concept. It was because Coné believed that his work as the CLO was done." That got me thinking, so I started checking around and sure enough, Coné is not alone. The CLOs of several other companies have also recently left their posts, and their positions have yet to be filled. Now that seems odd, since the last time I checked, firms were not eliminating the role of the chief information officer (CIO), general counsel, or vice president of HR.

On the related issue of job security and upward mobility of the CLO position itself, although definitive statistics are hard to come by, anecdotal evidence suggests that these have been tough times for CLOs. A number have left their old posts, voluntarily or otherwise, and their career moves have generally been lateral—or worse. In short, the CLO position has generally not been a springboard for upward job mobility, indicating that CLOs have had a considerably tougher time achieving success recognition and career progression in their organizations than their colleagues in other corporate functions.

Lie #4: If You Want a Career in Corporate Learning, You Should Want to Be a CLO.

On the contrary! Aspiring learning professionals should actually shoot *higher* than the title of CLO. Let me share an anecdote. I was recently called by an executive recruiter seeking suggestions for candidates who might be well suited for a *Fortune* 500 CLO opening that he was trying to fill. I asked the recruiter about the job specs for the position, and he shared with me a number of characteristics primarily associated with the functional skills of a senior education executive. The job specs included experience in individual and organizational needs assessment, competency modeling, all aspects of training and development, learning technologies, executive group facilitation, action learning, team and organization effectiveness, process engineering, consulting practices, and change management. In short, the job specs included all the relevant experience one might amass working up through the ranks of a traditional training and development organization.

Now don't get me wrong: These are all necessary and important skills, but they are far from sufficient to succeed as a CLO of a large organization in today's challenging business environment. So I told my recruiter friend that his client might be better served by a CLO who also demonstrates a clear understanding of the key business drivers and profit levers of the corporation, has a truly global mindset, proves his or her experience with delivering business results, and has an established track record in running a business entity, strong executive presence, communication skills, and exceptionally strong leadership qualities. The recruiter replied that I must have misunderstood; he was looking for a CLO, not a CEO, whom he thought would better fit the job characteristics I had just described. I responded that in my view, many of the requirements of the jobs are similar. Without strong management and leadership skills, neither a CLO nor a CEO is likely to succeed in their mission.

All this got me thinking: If many of the underlying professional attributes of these two positions are similar, how many of today's CEOs had started their careers (or at least passed through the position) as a CLO? As far as I can tell, the learning profession has never served as a training ground or springboard for topmost executive leadership. It doesn't appear that the career prospects of CLOs are likely to change much over the next decade. At a CLO symposium, I asked the audience members to comment on their prospects for future promotion to the top spot in their organizations. In response to the question: "How likely is it that you or your CLO will be promoted to CEO within the next 10 years?" none responded "very or somewhat likely." This is in contrast to 39 percent who said, "not in my lifetime!" These learning practitioners are to be commended for their honesty and candor if not their career progression prospects.

Now some readers might be thinking that the very question posed here is presumptuous in that as a dedicated learning practitioner, you may never have aspired to become a CEO. Fair enough. During my research, however, I discovered some interesting facts about where CEOs do come from, which is something learning professionals might want to consider. The list of leaders in the fields of retail, finance, telecommunications, and transportation who progressed to the CEO position through their CIO organization includes John Reed (Citigroup), David Bernauer (Walgreen's), Jacob Schorr (Spirit Airlines), Bob Martin (Walmart International), and Christopher Lofgren (Schneider National).

Looking further, I found numerous cases in which CEOs were promoted to the top spot from other corporate staff positions as well. For example, Dick Parsons, CEO of Time Warner, last served his company as the head of HR. The CEOs at Monsanto and U.S. Steel were promoted to the top spot from the position of general counsel. Of course, the chief financial officer (CFO) post has been the springboard for dozens of CEOs, including Richard Wagoner at General Motors and Hank McKinnell at Pfizer.

These findings, therefore, only reinforced my question about what is it about the learning profession that prevented it from achieving the full stature, respect, and upward mobility that many other organizational functions already have. My hypothesis may hold the key for many CLOs to improve the effectiveness of their corporate learning program—and perhaps even enhance their own career prospects.

To draw some lessons learned from analogous business functions, let's take a look at the evolving role of CIOs. Although the CIO to CEO jump may not seem so unusual now, such a career progression would have been unthinkable 20 or 30 years ago. In the 1970s, CIOs, or management information system (MIS) directors as they were more often known, were mostly technocrats who provided the care and feeding of the corporation's technology infrastructure. In short, they were technically focused and highly reactive in their dealings across the enterprise. Managers serving in this capacity were hardly well suited or positioned to jump to executive leadership.

The role of the CIO has changed dramatically over the ensuing two decades. The strategic role of technology changed within the corporation and, with it, so too did the role of the MIS director (figure 5-2). As technology became an integral driver of the corporation's overall business strategy and as information management became one of the company's most critical assets, the top technology executive, today's CIO, assumed a legitimate seat at the top management table in a far more proactive, business-oriented role.

CIOs played a pivotal role in delivering the remarkable improvement in industrial labor productivity cited earlier by successfully implementing large-scale technology systems that dramatically improved manufacturing worker productivity. Starting with material resource planning (MRP) systems in the 1960s, 1970s, and 1980s, and then progressing to enterprise resource planning systems in the 1990s, CIOs emerged at the forefront of delivering outstanding business results. More recently, the focus has shifted to service worker productivity, as exemplified by the technology enabling United Parcel Service and FedEx to reliably deliver and track hundreds of millions of packages per

Figure 5-2. Evolution of the CIO role.

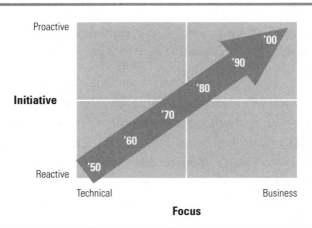

year. Backed by such success, what once may have seemed unthinkable no longer seemed so extraordinary. Indeed, the record of upward CIO mobility validates that this reward for performance did occur.

What can the learning profession realize from this? Many learning practitioners are in the same boat now that CIOs were in about 25 years ago. They are perceived as technocrats rather than proactive, business leaders within their enterprise. As Peter Drucker noted, the next opportunity for breakthrough business performance now rests on a company's ability to get more out of their knowledge workforce. As such, CLOs now have a unique opportunity to make a breakthrough contribution similar to what propelled many CIOs to success over the past several years. If more learning practitioners focused on driving breakthrough business value, it would not be unreasonable or unprecedented to aspire to higher executive stature in their organizations.

In many ways, achieving breakthrough improvements in knowledge worker performance is more difficult than enhancing production and transaction worker productivity. The reason is that the nature of knowledge work is more complex and heavily reliant on skills that were not readily conformable, such as high-level business judgment. CLOs must bring new skills to the opportunity and need at hand, namely a deep grasp of the value levers of the business, an understanding of the enabling skills required in mission critical workforces, and an ability to drive innovative and creative learning solutions that motivate superior business outcomes.

This view of the CLO as a critical driver of business outcomes calls for a new breed of professional. The recruiter's job spec noted earlier is a case in point of an organization perpetuating an outdated view of the

CLOs now have a unique opportunity to make a breakthrough contribution similar to what propelled many CIOs to success over the past several years. If more learning practitioners focused on driving breakthrough business value, it would not be unreasonable or unprecedented to aspire to higher executive stature in their organizations.

learning profession as strictly a specialist technocracy with a high likelihood of self-fulfilling and unsatisfying results.

There is an alternative, however. As an organizational entity, corporate universities are still relatively new in the game. Although the CEO promotion track may seem out of reach for many in the learning profession today, there are still ways to advance their careers. If practitioners complete the journey from functional specialist to becoming a proactive, value creator within the organization, the stature and the career prospects of CLOs will grow considerably. The challenge and opportunity are to make this journey more rapidly than the 30 years it took to transform the role of CIO.

To understand the desired role of the CLO, it is instructive to review the evolution of corporate education up to this point (figure 5-3). Two decades ago, corporate education was enjoying a renaissance, where it seemed that every company had or was establishing a corporate university and anointing a new class of executive known as the CLO. In fact, the number of corporate universities increased nearly fivefold during the period between 1987 and 2000, from 400 to more than 1,800 (Meister, 2000).

It's interesting to ask where these corporate universities came from. What were their charters and goals? After all, it's not as if training wasn't occurring in these companies before they established corporate universities. In retrospect, many companies merely went through the motions of renaming the "same old, same old" training function. But, for other

Figure 5-3. The evolution of corporate education.

Renaissance 1985-2001	Retrenchment 2001-2003	Legitimacy? 2004
• Rapid emergence of Corporate U's	• Intense	• Tipping point
• Creation of CLO position	• Budget	• Opportunity and need to legitimize the role of learning as a strategic enabler of business outcome
• Growth of budgets and staff	• Decentralization of business unit: "secession" from corporate universities	
• Lots of hype	• Selective closure of corporate universities	

companies, the creation of corporate universities signaled that they were raising the bar on how education would be managed, delivered, and tracked across the enterprise. The promise was that training would move out from behind the curtains to a highly visible and contributing element of a company's core competence.

Therefore, it was with great promise that the renaissance era of corporate universities ushered in so many new organizations with such high ambition. So how did we get from there to now, where some pundits are openly questioning whether the days of the CLO and their corporate universities are over? For one thing, a period of unprecedented uncertainty and corporate retrenchment ensued, punctuated by the unthinkable tragedy on 9/11. In the aftermath of these events, once again corporate education often became one of the first and most inviting targets for budget cutters across the enterprise. The official statistics suggest that U.S. corporate training outlays declined by 3 percent between 2001 and 2002 and dropped again by a similar amount in 2003. Nevertheless, many learning practitioners can attest that these statistics of single-digit percentage decreases in total training spend don't fully capture the decline in stature and influence that corporate learning executives felt during this era.

Therefore, there must be some other factors at play to explain why a profession with so much promise and impact could attract so much scrutiny and be asked once again to justify its existence. In fact, this question leads to the third and current era in the recent history of corporate education. In many ways, the corporate learning function is currently at a crossroads—a tipping point—that will define its direction for many years to come. In retrospect, the 1990s were probably overly exuberant, with aspirations for the strategic deployment of corporate education that exceeded both the capability and the capacity of most organizations. To be sure, the retrenchment of the past few years also does not represent normal times. Perhaps the pendulum has swung too far one way at first, and too far the other more recently. But, we are where we are, and the decisions made going forward will determine whether CLOs ultimately fulfill their potential to become contributing drivers of superior business and financial performance or if they will continue to decline in influence, stature, and perhaps even existence.

Lie #5: A CLO Effectively Manages the Delivery of Training in the Corporate University.

Although I wouldn't call this premise a lie per se, there are, nonetheless, two notable problems with this description of the CLO's job that go beyond mere semantics. The first is the common belief that the basic function of the CLO is training. *Merriam-Webster* defines training as "to form by instruction, discipline, or drill...so as to make fit, qualified, or proficient." Defined as such, training connotes a rote, procedural approach that may teach basic levels of proficiency but not necessarily the high-level business judgment and competence that are critical to superior workforce performance in today's knowledge economy.

In contrast to the dictionary definition of learning is this one: modification of a behavioral tendency by experience. The emphasis here goes beyond training the skills to know how to perform a given task, to the mastery and business judgment to know when and which relevant skills should be applied to achieve the best outcome in dynamically changing situations. As an example, consider the corporate learning challenge for customer service representatives (CSRs). The learning (not training) objective here goes beyond teaching CSRs how to follow rote, computer-generated telephone scripts, to developing the judgment to effectively respond to the unique circumstances of each individual customer. There is considerable evidence to attest that effective learning programs can measurably improve CSR performance, which, in turn, translates into higher levels of customer satisfaction, loyalty, and higher corporate profitability (Heskett, Sasser, & Schlesinger, 2003). Thus, the challenge and payoff from delivering superior learning far exceeds the impact of most traditional training programs.

To put a punctuation point on this issue, I would argue that training is something better directed toward our household pets than to our corporate colleagues! Wherever possible, use of the term "training" should be banished from the job description of the CLO.

Another concern relates to the widespread use of the term "corporate university" to describe the umbrella organization led by CLOs. Think back to the last time you attended a formal university—presumably when you received your undergraduate or graduate degree. If you're like many students, your fondest memories from that era relate to the carefree, sheltered educational cocoon that university life allowed, and, one hopes, the intellectual stimulation provided by a few memorable professors. In contrast, the experience of dealing with university administration is likely to conjure up far darker memories of rules, regulations, and unresponsive bureaucracy.

With these common associations in mind, does the term corporate university conjure up the type of organization that successful CLOs should want to lead in a business environment? I would suggest that a better alternative is for corporate learning organizations to leave their ivory towers behind and become far more imbedded in the fabric of their corporation's business. For example, General Electric's Jack Welch Leadership Center and British Telecom's Retail Centre of Excellence are aligned strongly with the desired business outcome of their respective enterprises in more than just the name.

Broadly speaking, this view gets to the heart of the proper role and aspirations for a successful CLO. There are three key success factors for effective CLOs:

➤ Establish appropriate infrastructure, standards, and procedures to ensure the delivery of measurably effective learning across the global enterprise.

➤ Serve as a strategic enabler of business outcomes.

➤ Continually innovate to enhance value delivered through high-performance workforces.

The first key success factor, establishing appropriate infrastructure, standards, and procedures, lays the foundation enabling effective learning to be delivered across the global extended enterprise. Specific examples include

➤ fully deploying a workforce competency model and a supporting curriculum across all major job functions

➤ implementing an enterprisewide, robust learning management system accessible 24 hours a day, seven days a week to all employees

➤ converting the majority of available courses, wherever appropriate, to e-learning formats, and supporting flexible hybrid learning models

> ➤ rigorously measuring the impact of all training on business outcomes

> ➤ deploying workforce certification programs across all corporate business units.

Developing and deploying these capabilities across the enterprise provides the basis to achieve the second key success factor of the CLO's job: to serve as a strategic enabler of business outcomes. Examples include supporting aggressive speed to market targets for new product launches, enhancing corporate-wide adoption of Six Sigma processes, stimulating revenue growth through effective customer education programs, aligning supply chain processes through supplier learning initiatives, and spearheading leadership development programs. The point here is that there are significant learning enablers associated with every major strategic initiative within the enterprise. Successful CLOs must ensure that their organizations are proactively involved in delivering the requisite learning capabilities. In addition, it's necessary that the business outcomes of the enabling learning initiatives are rigorously measured, reported, and used as a basis to continually improve the impact of corporate learning across the enterprise.

Finally, successful CLOs should serve as a focal point for incubating new ideas and implementing innovative approaches for leadership and workforce capability development. The intent here is to continually improve the technologies and processes used for employee, customer, and supplier education while also enhancing the effectiveness of knowledge management, performance support, collaboration tools, change management, and leadership development. The opportunity is to move beyond delivering training within the confines of the corporate university to consistently enable critical business outcomes across the enterprise.

Lie #6: If the CEO Does Not Support Learning, There's Little the CLO Can Do to Maximize Corporate Education.

When Jack Welch recruited Noel Tichy as the head of management education at General Electric (GE) in 1985, Welch had already committed to use corporate education as the focal point for a broad-based strategy and culture change within the venerable enterprise. Over the next several years, Tichy and his CLO successors made admirable progress. They revitalized Crotonville to become one of the premier corporate learning centers in the world. Their accomplishments included

➤ championing action learning based on actual GE business situations to replace the use of generic case studies and textbook curricula

➤ pioneering innovative e-learning applications, including some of the most sophisticated business simulation applications ever developed

➤ serving as a showcase for legions of CLOs looking to benchmark corporate education best practices.

Throughout his illustrious 23-year career as CEO of GE, Jack Welch remained committed to corporate education, returning to Crotonville twice a month to share his teachable point of view with thousands of managers across the global enterprise. Despite his prodigious accomplishments as a business executive and his reputation for being one of the best CEOs in history, Welch thought of himself, first and foremost, as a teacher. Though most business historians feel that Welch's commitment to corporate education was a major contributor to the firm's unparalleled success, few CEOs have similarly embraced Welch's passion for corporate learning within their own enterprises.

How can a CLO achieve significant business impact within his or her firm absent the strong support of executive leadership? To better understand this issue, a couple of years ago I surveyed a representative sample of 150 CLOs and senior learning professionals on what were the most significant challenges holding them back from improving the effectiveness of their corporate learning program (Accenture, 2002). I fully expected that financial constraints would head the list of responses by a long shot. After all, what corporate learning organization could possibly believe it has a budget sufficient to meet the growing demands of its organization?

As shown in figure 5-4, budget constraints did indeed rank as the most frequent response, but just barely. This category was cited by about half the respondents as one of the two biggest constraints to improving the effectiveness of the corporate learning agenda. Following just behind were two indicators of the stature and support of the learning organization within the enterprise. About 46 percent of respondents noted that the lack of sufficient acceptance across the global enterprise was one of the two main constraints against better performance. A related issue is shown by the 31 percent that noted the lack of adequate executive sponsorship within their learning organization. The other notable category, cited by 35 percent, was a lack of skills and management depth in the learning organization itself.

These results suggest that in too many organizations, CLOs are caught in lose–lose situations. They perceive that they lack adequate senior executive support, perhaps contributing to anemic funding for corporate education initiatives. Such constraints hamper their ability to build critical skills and management depth in the learning organization, which in turn compromises the effectiveness of learning outcomes delivered across the enterprise.

The question, therefore, is how to convert this self-perpetuating cycle of low support, which leads to low funding, which leads to low skills, which leads to low impact. Low impact directly links back to the

Figure 5-4. The greatest challenges facing CLOs.

What are the greatest challenges you face today in improving effectiveness of your corporate learning program?

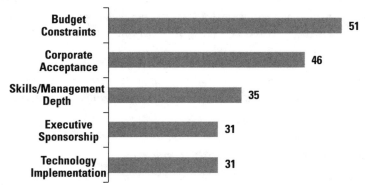

Source: Accenture, *CLO Symposium Survey,* 2002.

beginning of the cycle: low executive support. CLOs need to deliver significant, measurable value to the corporation and they need to do it consistently to secure executive support and initiate a positive support cycle. Certainly, it would be easier to live in this virtuous world if all CEOs shared Welch's passion for the learning profession.

Lie #6 claims that there is nothing a CLO can do to achieve maximized corporate education without executive backing. This premise is perhaps the most sinister lie of all for CLOs who hope to make a difference in their organizations. In truth, what's called for from CLOs in such circumstances is a heavy dose of leadership to set and achieve the critical objectives required to succeed, given the hand they've been dealt. It can be done.

Recall the earlier discussion about CIOs who transformed their IT departments into core enablers of their firm's value creation strategy. It's fair to assume that the early exemplars of this transition did not necessarily occur because, in the organizations in question, the CEO pulled the IT department up by its bootstraps. More likely, the ascendancy of IT as a strategic enabler was driven by a new breed of CIO who recognized and acted on the opportunity to create significant value within the enterprise, working collaboratively with business unit leaders to make it happen.

The lessons learned provide guidance on the road ahead for successful CLOs. My suggestion would be to start by looking from the outside in. There's still plenty to do inside your learning group to upgrade infrastructure, technology, and business processes. But, the most immediate need is to look outside the learning organization to your enterprise as a whole. Toward that end, CLOs should ask themselves four questions:

> *What are the most critical value creation priorities of my enterprise?* The answer to this question will vary, but most

---

CLOs need to deliver significant, measurable value to the corporation and they need to do it consistently to secure executive support and initiate a positive support cycle.

---

companies I deal with tend to put revenue generation at or near the top of the list, with a pressing interest in driving up the effectiveness and capabilities of the salesforce. Whether it is sales, global expansion, product development, or something else, there are undoubtedly clearly articulated strategic imperatives for your organization. These imperatives have an associated requirement for enabling improved workforce performance. Be sure you know where your company is focusing its efforts because your learning organization should align its priorities accordingly.

➤ *Is my learning organization hardwired into these strategic imperatives, and is it widely recognized as a critical enabler of the desired outcomes?* When convicted bank robber Willy Sutton was once asked why he robbed banks, he answered, "Because that's where the money is!" CLOs should think accordingly and focus the learning organization's efforts where the greatest value creation opportunities are. Unfortunately, in many companies the corporate learning function tends to focus primarily on foundational skill-building programs (figure 5-5). In such cases, the core business functions (for example, sales, product development) and P&L units drive their own formal learning programs. At an even higher level, major corporate initiatives—such as executive leadership development, customer-centricity, or firmwide Six Sigma programs—are often driven from the top, with little or no support from corporate learning. In this depicted hierarchy of learning opportunities, the highest potential for value creation exists at the top of the Parthenon, which is where CLOs mainly should be focused.

➤ *How can a learning organization get plugged into learning delivery at or above the pillars of the Parthenon, particularly in organizations where line executives have traditionally kept tight rein on "their" programs?* The answer lies in focus, persistence, and commitment to superior value delivery. In short, the CLO needs to earn the right to participate more broadly in the learning initiatives across the organization by bringing innovative value creating ideas to the table. In so doing,

Figure 5-5. The corporate learning Parthenon.

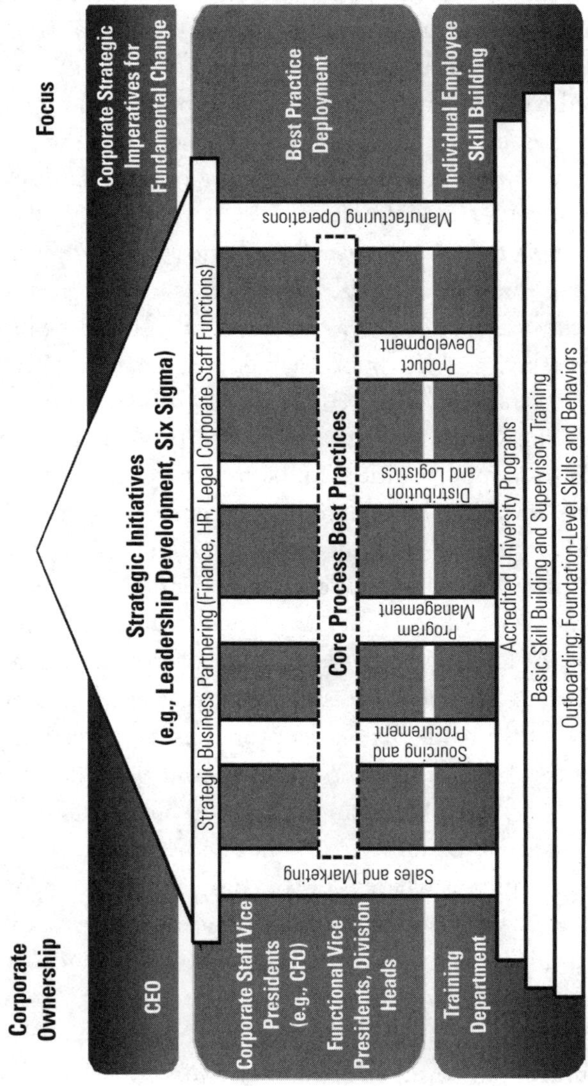

Corporate Ownership		Focus

Corporate Strategic Imperatives for Fundamental Change

Best Practice Deployment

Individual Employee Skill Building

Strategic Initiatives (e.g., Leadership Development, Six Sigma)

Strategic Business Partnering (Finance, HR, Legal Corporate Staff Functions)

Core Process Best Practices

Manufacturing Operations

Product Development

Distribution and Logistics

Program Management

Sourcing and Procurement

Sales and Marketing

CEO

Corporate Staff Vice Presidents (e.g., CFO)

Functional Vice Presidents, Division Heads

Training Department

Accredited University Programs

Basic Skill Building and Supervisory Training

Outboarding: Foundation-Level Skills and Behaviors

CLOs will need to pick their spots carefully. Not every business unit will be equally receptive to partnering with corporate learning and embracing new approaches. But by focusing on the right initiatives and consistently exceeding the firm's expectations for value delivery, the CLO can extend his or her influence across the organization over time. In short, successful CLOs need to create their own virtuous cycles. It starts with value delivered, leading to increased demand for learning services across the enterprise, accompanied by increased funding availability, enabling the continual improvement of management depth and technological innovation within the learning organization. Creating this virtuous cycle, particularly absent a CEO mandate for change, calls for strong leadership on the part of the CLO. Those that are up to this task are exactly the kind of executives that can not only deliver superior learning value to their companies, but demonstrate the leadership attributes required to aspire to even higher levels of corporate responsibility.

➤ *Do I have the tools and capabilities at my disposal to deliver breakthrough performance improvements?* Of course, the virtuous cycle noted above can only occur if the learning organization has the capabilities to deliver and continually improve superior learning value. For many organizations, this highlights the need to upgrade the infrastructure, processes, and procedures to ensure the delivery of measurably effective learning across the global enterprise.

Overcoming the Lies With Truth

The bottom line is that CLOs have the need and opportunity to deliver considerably higher value to their organizations. Those up to the challenge of making knowledge work considerably more productive can truly unlock what Peter Drucker (1978, p. 290) called "the great management task of this century." Surely, this is an aspiration worthy of a CLO's passion, vision, and leadership.

The Lie	The Truth
CLOs have a seat at the management table.	The CLO function is not currently performing anywhere near its potential and will not do so, absent a more radical change agenda driven by a new breed of CLO.
Executives don't understand the value of effective corporate training.	Workforce performance is perceived as a critical strategic need by CEOs in most corporations. So, learning organizations have a tremendous opportunity to assume more leadership in deploying innovative, impacting, and relevant workforce improvement programs.
A CLO's role is as important as any other corporate function.	The CLO position has generally not been a springboard for upward job mobility, suggesting that CLOs have had a considerably tougher time achieving success recognition and career progression in their organizations than their colleagues in other corporate functions.
If you want a career in corporate learning, you should want to be a CLO.	Aspiring learning professionals should actually shoot *higher* than the title of CLO. The decisions made going forward will determine whether CLOs ultimately fulfill their potential to become a contributing driver of superior business and financial performance or if they will continue to decline in influence, stature, and perhaps even existence.
A CLO effectively manages the delivery of training in the corporate university.	The opportunity is to move beyond delivering training within the confines of the corporate university to consistently enabling critical business outcomes across the enterprise by incubating new ideas and implementing innovative approaches for leadership and workforce capability development.
If the CEO does not support learning, there's little the CLO can do to maximize corporate education.	This is perhaps the most sinister lie of all for CLOs who hope to make a difference in their organizations. In truth, what's called for from CLOs is a heavy dose of leadership to set and achieve the critical objectives required to succeed, given the hand they've been dealt. It can be done.

References

Accenture. (2003, January). *The High Performance Workforce Study.*

————. (2002). *CLO Symposium Survey.*

Chief Learning Officer Business Intelligence Board. (2005). *The 2005 Chief Learning Officer Business Intelligence Industry Report.* http://www.clomedia.com.

Drucker, P. (2002). *Managing in the Next Society.* New York: Truman Talley Books/St. Martin's Griffin.

————. (1978). *The Age of Discontinuity: Guidelines to Our Changing Society.* New York: Harper & Row.

Gale, S.F. (2003, October). "For Some Chief Learning Officers, One of the Goals is Job Insecurity." *Workforce Management.* http://www.workforce.com.

Heskett, J.L., W.D. Sasser, and L.A. Schlesinger. (2003). *The Value Profit Chain.* New York: Free Press.

Meister, J. (2000, September 15). "The Role of Web-Based Education: Testimony Before Web-Based Education Commission." http://www.hpcnet.org/cgi-bin/global/a_bus_card.cgi?SiteID=179527.

Pringle, D. (2003, January 7). "Learning Gurus Adapt to Escape Corporate Axes." *Wall Street Journal,* B1.

Lies About Consultants and Vendors

Charlene J. Zeiberg

Back in the late 1990s during the Internet boom, I worked for a large financial services company, charged with the firm's venture into the world of e-learning. I had been promoted recently and given the charge to lead the organization into the promised land of learning, where learning is served up to each employee's desktop, providing just what he or she needed, exactly when it was needed. As a seasoned training and learning professional, I was up for this exciting challenge.

After determining the organization's needs, I concluded that delivering learning to thousands of employees' desktops would require a learning management system (LMS). After scouring the marketplace and examining almost every system out there (this was the preconsolidation e-learning marketplace where there were at least triple the number of systems that exist today), I initiated a thorough request-for-proposal process, resulting in the selection of an up-and-coming, somewhat respected LMS vendor. (I say "somewhat respected" because at that time there were many unknowns about the technology and no vendor had a flawless record.)

The vendor I selected was exceptionally eager to add a large financial services company to its cadre of clients; it was on the verge of going public and this sale would be a feather in its cap. I felt confident about my decision, which was a visible and expensive one, partly because of the relationship I developed with the account executive, Tom. I trusted Tom and believed that he had been forthright throughout the business development process. What I didn't know was what lurked above him in his organization.

Immediately after I awarded the business to the vendor, Tom informed me that his manager, Frank, the vice president of global sales, would be contacting me. I presumed that he wanted to thank me for my business. When Frank called, he shared all the niceties that one would expect. Then he proceeded with the true reason for his call: He asked if we could quickly sign the contract and cut a check for the investment outlined in their proposal. He indicated that the initial public offering (IPO) was imminent and that this sale would help make their numbers for the quarter. I don't know if I was more floored by the complete and utter directness of the request (as there was absolutely no finesse) or by his chutzpah.

Call it spite, but after the conversation, I didn't help the contract process move any faster than normal. My firm was not on the vendor client list in time for the vendor's IPO. Tom was embarrassed and profusely apologized to me. Frank had initially asked Tom to do the dirty work, but he had refused. When Frank said he would make the call, Tom warned him that doing so would risk the business and the client relationship. Frank was clearly more concerned with trying to pull in large-firm name recognition and making his target. Tom and I remain friends and business colleagues, but we still get a chuckle about this situation.

So why am I, a consultant, writing about the lies and antics of vendors and consultants? Having headed up a variety of learning and training functions and having worked as a consultant for a major training firm and now as an independent consultant, I can lend a balanced perspective on the topic. When I was on the inside, my expectations of consultants were very high and often unrealistic. Now I spend my time trying to live up to these very same expectations. It always fascinates me when I see vendors living these lies, and I am continually baffled as to what keeps them in business.

Many learning professionals consider consultants a necessary evil, whereas others have had rewarding consultant partnerships. Some of you may fall somewhere in the middle, being cautiously optimistic about your vendor relationships. So, it goes without saying that the lies I share with you are not universal or meant to be stereotypes. They are standard complaints that I have heard as a client or that my clients have shared with me. These lies are generalized statements or proclamations that have been made by some vendors; they are presented here for your consideration. I hope that these revelations will lead to more productive vendor alliances and partnerships.

Many learning professionals consider consultants a necessary evil, whereas others have had rewarding consultant partnerships. Some of you may fall somewhere in the middle, being cautiously optimistic about your vendor relationships.

Lie #1: This Team of Experienced Consultants Will Be Engaged on This Project.

Does this sound familiar? While engaging a vendor for an important project you decided to outsource, you meet with several of the vendor's consultants who are part of the proposed project team. You are impressed with the team members, and you particularly like their experience within your industry, demonstrated knowledge of the content, level of creativity, and the overall chemistry with your organization. After awarding the business to this vendor and launching the project, the faces suddenly change. You may see one familiar face, but the other project team members are consultants whom you have never seen before. Overall, the team is more junior than the seasoned team originally presented to you.

This scenario is all too common when dealing with a vendor. Usually the vendor does not intend to do the old bait and switch, but changes in team members are, unfortunately, sometimes unavoidable when allocating resources among client projects. When I was consulting, I was frequently involved in the business development process and asked to consult with and wow prospective clients. I never knew if I would actually work on the project if we were to win the business. Many times, I attended prospective client meetings knowing I would not be available for the project. Because of the lag in the business development process, chances are that by the time a vendor wins the business, the proposed team resources may be fully engaged on other client projects. If only I had $100 for each meeting I attended and every proposal in which my bio appeared!

So, what can you do to prevent situations like this and ensure that you secure the consulting resources you want? The best you can do is express your concern, ask pointed questions, and let the vendor's representatives know that although you are potentially engaging their company, you are really selecting the team of consultants who have the expertise you require. Be sure to ask these questions:

> Will this be the team dedicated to my project from start to finish?
> Is there anyone on the team that may have a conflicting client project and is potentially not available?
> What can you do to guarantee the availability of the team you presented?
> If you need to substitute team members, who would you consider? Can you share their résumés?
> Will I have the opportunity to approve the new team members you select? (This shouldn't really be a question, but, rather, a contractual requirement.)

Maybe you won't get all the answers you want, but at the very least you have put your vendors on notice that casual resource swapping is something that you won't tolerate. You might be surprised at how expressing your views on this subject can influence your vendor's decisions about assigning your project's resources.

Lie #2: The Training Materials Will Be Custom Built for You.

When I worked for a well-known training consulting firm, this was a common statement. Most of the more notable training vendors who provide training content have an arsenal of generic content sitting on a shelf waiting to be called into battle. In some cases, this generic content was created based on best-practice research the vendor conducted. In other cases, the content, which was based on no research at all, was left over from previous client engagements.

Many times when a client requests a customized program from the vendor, generic content is manipulated, massaged, repackaged, or updated, but very little custom content is actually created. The customized part of the program is often nothing more than a replacement of terms (for example, employee instead of staff member or motivational feedback instead of positive feedback). You get the idea. Maybe there is a single custom case study or role play developed, or perhaps the client's competency model is inserted into the materials and referred to occasionally. Regardless, it is a stretch to call any of this work custom.

It is important to understand the distinction between custom materials and tailored materials. A custom program should be built from the ground up. A tailored program builds upon generic or previously used program content and modifies it in some fashion, as in the examples above. Many training vendors will charge you a fortune to perform these simple replacements they have labeled as "custom."

Be sure to determine if your programs require tailoring or customization and ask vendors specific questions to understand how they will arrive at the final work product. Consider asking:

➤ Will you be designing this program and writing all new content or will you leverage your existing content?
➤ May I review your generic training materials on this topic?
➤ What will you do to tailor the content? How does this affect our ownership or licensing arrangement?

One of my clients hired a well-known training consulting firm to design, develop, and deliver a management development program. The client believed that the program would be customized for the organization and its culture. I was involved as a consultant working on another part of this initiative but was asked to work with the new vendor to make sure that the work was consistent. Knowing the vendor's content fairly well, it was obvious to me that nothing more than a few terms and concepts were replaced with different terms and concepts, an inexpensive word-processing task. When my client shared with me the $20,000 bill paid for this so-called custom project, I knew the work was hardly worth the price tag.

Tailoring may meet your specific needs, but make sure you are clear on the distinction because of implications regarding ownership of the content, bringing me to the next lie.

Lie #3: You Will Own Everything We Build for You.

This lie is a typical response to the question on ownership. Ownership depends on a couple of factors:

> ➤ Was the content customized, in the true sense of the word, for your organization?
> ➤ Was off-the-shelf content or the vendor's intellectual capital leveraged to create your program?
> ➤ Did the vendor create any unique case studies, role plays, or content specific to your organization?

The general rule is that the more development work that is performed from the ground up for your project, the more you own outright. Keeping this rule in mind, let's dissect the lie that is the subject of this section. Where is the emphasis placed in each of these statements?

> ➤ "You will own *everything* we build for you."
> ➤ "You will own everything *we build* for you."

Depending on where the emphasis is placed, the meaning of this sentence changes substantially. You, as the client, are hoping that the vendor has expressed your ownership rights based on the first example; you will exclusively own everything the vendor builds for you. However, it is more likely that the vendor's intention is reflected in the second example: You will own everything the vendor built exclusively for you.

This links back to Lie #2. Chances are that the content you thought was built especially for you is really the vendor's intellectual capital tailored for your needs and, therefore, you do not have *any* ownership rights. The only content you own outright is the development work for hire, such as case studies, role plays, or paragraphs of content inserted into workbooks or PowerPoint slides. (Some vendors won't even give you those!)

The recent trend is for clients to own all deliverables, giving them the freedom to alter and duplicate program content without cost. Without ownership, you are required to pay per-participant licensing fees, which can be costly—up to $500 per learner for a classroom program, or you have to pay charges for rights to print or rights to use, allowing you to print and distribute a specific number of program materials. The financial benefits of ownership are obvious.

If ownership is a concern for you and your organization, be sure to discuss it explicitly with the vendor and ask:

> ➤ What will we own and have the right to alter, duplicate, and distribute free of charge?
> ➤ What do you (the vendor) own? What are the fees associated with our use of this content? Are there any restrictions on the use of this content?
> ➤ How will the copyright on the content be treated? Will the vendor own it, will we, or will it be shared?
> ➤ What can be done during the design and development process to ensure our ownership?

Determine your ownership requirements early in the negotiation process. Some vendors are more flexible than others are. The vendor's position on this issue depends somewhat on its investment in conducting best practice research and in creating proprietary intellectual capital, which brings me to Lie #4.

Lie #4: Our Work Is Based on Best Practice Research.

Many learning and training vendors invest in best practice research, which involves mining the specific practices, actions, and behaviors that lead to high performance. These vendors tend to be more expensive because of the overhead required to keep research fresh and current with trends in the business environment. For some organizations, this research provides credibility for both the vendor and the learning experience. It acts as the catalyst for change, giving leaders, managers, sales representatives, and customer service providers a reason for change based on the current best practices for optimal performance. Others, because the research is not specific to their organization, may consider the findings irrelevant to their organization's role, industry, or culture.

If research is important to you and your organization, you need to accept the top quality and premium costs associated with it. Engage the vendor in a discussion regarding its research philosophy and approach by asking:

> ➤ What guides your research agenda?
> ➤ How does the research conducted relate to my project and goals?
> ➤ Can you tell me about the research base and whether it's applicable to my industry?
> ➤ How recent is the research?
> ➤ How often is the research updated?
> ➤ Will you provide me with new content based on the updates?

Organizations tend to value organization development research as they attempt to base their programs on the latest and greatest studies dealing with how to achieve greatness. Frankly, not all research is created equal, nor is it always relevant to your organization and industry. Be sure to examine the suitability of the research before making it the underpinning of your learning initiative.

Lie #5: We Use a Reliable Project Management Process.

Did you ever have a vendor project that was totally disorganized—one that couldn't even be classified as organized chaos because there was no apparent project management approach or methodology to guide the team's work? Perhaps the roles and responsibilities were not defined or the project plans lacked detail or contingency planning.

This was my concern as a client when I needed to outsource projects. I had the expectation, and still do, that vendors should have a more sound and more dynamic project management process than I could employ myself, one that accounts for every task and interdependency. Unfortunately, I have found that this so-called reliable project management process is not all that reliable.

What should you expect and how can you ensure that the vendor has an effective approach to managing your project? Their approach should include

> ➤ clear roles and responsibilities
> ➤ client resource requirements (for example, a project leader, subject matter experts [SMEs], review teams)
> ➤ ground rules for working together

➤ a detailed project plan organized by phase/stream of work (or deliverable) with detailed tasks and assigned resources

➤ contingency plans to account for a variety of what-if scenarios in case task deadlines are not met

➤ process for identifying client review teams

➤ client review procedures

➤ regularly scheduled status calls

➤ escalation processes

➤ communication standards

➤ file-naming conventions

➤ process for determining out-of-scope activities.

To ensure that a solid project management approach exists, you should ask the vendor:

➤ Can you give me an example of a similar client project and how it was managed?

➤ Can you provide me with a sample project plan and the project management templates you will use?

➤ May I speak to a couple of your clients to discuss how their projects were managed?

If your project is global, an important element of the project management process is the seamless implementation across the enterprise. Many vendors claim that they can orchestrate this type of initiative—another potential lie or exaggeration that is the subject of the next section.

Lie #6: We Can Support a Global Rollout.

Global learning is no longer a strategy; it's a requirement. One challenge is to deliver consistent practices and performance across very different cultures. At some point, if it hasn't happened already, you will need to orchestrate the global rollout of a key learning initiative.

There will be much to manage, and every vendor will claim to be ready, willing, and able to assist you. Vendors use terms such as global presence or global expertise to describe their capabilities. The truth is that many learning vendors can support global implementation. It is the extent and expense of that support that is the question.

Global learning is no longer a strategy; it's a requirement.

Essential to your success is the ability of your learning and consulting solutions to retain core consistency with subtle adaptation to ensure relevance and impact in different cultures. Before you determine the vendor's global capabilities, you need to determine your own needs and requirements by asking:

➤ Are you seeking global best practice research to inform your initiative? A globally adaptive approach can ingrain core concepts consistent with global strategy.

➤ Do you, for coordination and management purposes, require the vendor to have presence in the countries you are targeting?

➤ Do program materials or online content need multiple languages or dialects? Are materials written in English acceptable or must the materials be produced in different languages to maximize learning. Keep in mind that for programs that truly are custom, you will probably need to absorb the cost for translating and checking for cultural appropriateness.

➤ If it is a classroom-based program, does the program need to be facilitated in multiple languages?

➤ Must instructors be in close proximity of the delivery location or resident in the countries you will be targeting?

➤ Must the program be delivered synchronously or is it acceptable to use asynchronous technology so that time differences are not an important factor?

Vendors that are truly global typically have

➤ satellite offices and strategic partnerships located around the world

➤ global best practice research

➤ programs (classroom and online) that are tailored to a variety of cultures with culturally relevant examples, modified approaches to fit local norms and pace, and materials in multiple languages or dialects

➤ resident facilitators, skilled in multiple native languages and dialects, around the globe.

You may find yourself attracted to a potential vendor that can support your global initiative without being truly global. This may be a concession you are willing to make.

Lie #7: Our Online Content Will Easily Integrate With Your Platform.

Every e-learning project has technical considerations to manage. It is very important to make sure that the online content you choose will operate in your technical environment and work on your employees' computers. The uncertainty about compatibility of online content with delivery systems such as LMSs and content management systems (CMSs) has been frustrating for both learning professionals and vendors. The lessons learned over the last decade underscore that you cannot take vendor statements about system compatibility at face value. You must do your homework to ensure compatibility.

With the advances in SCORM (a suite of technical standards that enable web-based learning systems to find, import, share, reuse, and export learning content in a standardized way), learning professionals have a basis for determining compatibility. Adherence to SCORM standards is essential for launching and tracking directed learning or training experiences, as well as defining the intended behavior and logic of these complex experiences.

Even with SCORM, compatibility is not guaranteed. The only way to ensure that your delivery system can serve up the content you require is to test, test, and test some more to check its compatibility. When looking at e-learning content:

➤ Learn about the vendor's approach to being SCORM compliant.
➤ Determine if the vendor has clients with the same LMS/CMS that successfully use the vendor's content. Personally speak to these clients to learn from their challenges.
➤ Test the content on your own delivery systems.

Despite your best efforts, be prepared to face challenges during the implementation process. Consider the process a learning experience and sometimes a game of chance.

Lie #8: Clients Never Tell Lies.

Up to this point, I have focused on lies clients might hear from vendors. It would only be fair if I also shared some of the lies that vendors hear from learning professionals. However, calling these statements lies is probably extreme; many of these come out of the client's optimistic nature and overeager willingness to assist the vendor. These are, in essence, cautions to vendors about client statements that have the potential to lead to trouble.

We Have an Executive Sponsor for This Project.

Most vendors agree that when a project starts, there often is no committed executive sponsor. Although the client organization may have identified the sponsor, the individual is probably not yet engaged in the initiative and committed to it with support and buy-in.

We Have the Budget Required for This Project.

It is very common for the client organization to determine its budget in the absence of any competitive pricing information from vendors. To a vendor's dismay, many times, the desired solution is totally unrealistic given the available funding. It would be helpful if the project budget could be shared with the vendor to help it craft a realistic solution that fits the client's budget.

The counter-argument is, of course, that vendors will propose solutions that spend every cent of the budget even if not necessary to achieve the objective. There is no easy answer to this one, other than to work with vendors whom you trust.

We are Ready to Start the Project.

Hurry up and wait! Sometimes clients think they're ready to initiate a project, but they are missing some essential elements for a successful project launch and vendor partnership. For example, the following are necessary for an effective project launch:

➤ executive sponsorship
➤ determination of approach
➤ relevant materials needed by the vendor
➤ time to dedicate to the launch of the project

➤ established purchase order
➤ availability of SMEs
➤ dedicated internal project manager.

Have the vendor create a project plan that outlines key project tasks and deadlines. Carefully review the plan to make sure it's realistic. Consider such issues as

➤ When am I on vacation or out of the office and unable to review or approve documents, who will step in?
➤ Who else needs to review it? Will they be available to meet deadlines?

Have a list of SMEs who can help when you need it. Ask your SMEs if they have the time to help. Brief them on the project and determine with them if they are the right people or if someone else would be better.

The Design Is Complete and There Are No Additional Changes.
Make sure that all required parties—including stakeholders, SMEs, and your manager—have reviewed and signed off on any design or strategy documents. Because the design serves as the blueprint for other deliverables, changes, even the most minor, can result in repercussions throughout the project that can cost time and money.

This Project Must Be Completed by the End of February.
Having deadlines is important, but making them too tight can compromise the quality of the project. Evaluate the importance of the project relative to the time you realistically have to complete it. Many project delays are caused not by vendor delays but by clients who are not able to fulfill their responsibilities. Vendors rely on client activities for moving forward. It is better for the vendor to be waiting for you than for you to wait for the vendor.

I Can Make That Decision.
Be sure this is the case before you mutter these words. What will happen when you share your decision with your manager or internal client? Is it a minor detail or something that he or she will have an

opinion about? Even if you have the authority to make the decision, others may provide you with feedback that will reverse the decision and erode your credibility.

I'll Get on That Right Away.

Before you make any promises to provide the vendor with needed materials or schedule meetings with SMEs, check your schedule and to-do list. If you really can't do it, think about delegating the task or moving the deadline. Ask consultants what they need to meet their deadlines before committing.

Overcoming the Lies With Truth

There is a correlation between the success or failure of a project and the quality of the vendor–client relationship. Although there is plenty to be skeptical about, approach the vendor relationship with optimism and openness. The partnership greatly depends on both parties disclosing their expectations and capabilities.

Vendors and clients are not always on the same page when it comes to discussing learning. Vendors might communicate vague capabilities while clients speak of vague needs and outcomes. Vendors and clients are not purposely trying to confuse each other or complicate the relationship; each has a different knowledge base and perspective. Understanding each other's perspective will aid in establishing a mutually beneficial relationship. When you select a vendor or consultant, be sure you know and understand

- ➤ the scope of the deliverables
- ➤ the pricing structure for the project
- ➤ the dedicated project team members and their roles and responsibilities
- ➤ the vendor's project management process
- ➤ the level of customization and tailoring that will be provided
- ➤ who owns the materials and the rights associated with ownership
- ➤ the research, if any, that will be the basis for your project and its relevance and value

➤ the firm's global presence and capability

➤ what the vendor needs in regard to time commitment and resources.

Keep in mind the questions I've suggested along the way to help fortify your vendor–client relationships. Communicating within the relationship allows smoother transitions as the project advances from design to implementation to review. Remember that asking all the right questions won't always get you the answers you want to hear, but it will alert your partners that you are on top of things and make you aware of potential issues down the road.

The Lie	The Truth
This team of experienced consultants will be engaged on this project.	While engaging a vendor for an important project you decided to outsource, you meet with several of the vendor's consultants who are part of the proposed project team. Confirm that these are the consultants who will be assigned to the project once it begins.
The training materials will be custom built for you.	Because many firms create their content based on best practice research, they are not looking to build content for clients from the ground up but rather to leverage their investment in the creation of generic content. Most vendors look to tailor their existing content by making tweaks to some of the language and terms used.
You will own everything we build for you.	Chances are that the content you thought was built especially for you is really the vendor's intellectual capital tailored for your needs, and, therefore, you do not have any ownership rights. The only content you own outright is the development work for hire, such as case studies, role plays, or paragraphs of content inserted into workbooks or PowerPoint slides.
Our work is based on best practice research.	Frankly, not all research is created equal, nor is it always relevant to your organization and industry. Be sure first to examine the suitability of the research before making it the underpinning of your learning initiative.
We use a reliable project management process.	Many vendors claim that they can manage large-scale initiatives, but their process may not be as reliable as you hope and expect. Ask to review sample project plans and documents to confirm this capability.
We can support a global rollout.	Vendors define global capability in different terms. The vendor may truly believe it can support a global rollout, but it may not be to the extent that your organization requires.
Our online content will easily integrate with your platform.	Even with SCORM, compatibility is not guaranteed. The only way to ensure that your delivery system can serve up the content you require is to test, test, test, and then test some more.
Clients never tell lies.	Well, maybe they are really not lies but misconceptions or overstatements based on mainly good intentions. Clients are not purposely trying to complicate the relationship. Understanding each other's perspective will aid in establishing a mutually beneficial relationship.

Recommended Reading

Everett, J. (1998). "When Training Professionals Begin to Manage Vendors." In *Building Learning Capability Through Outsourcing (In Action Series)*, ed. M.C. Anderson. Alexandria, VA: ASTD Press.

Kruse, K. (2003, April). "Suppliers Are From Mars, Buyers Are From Venus." *Learning Circuits, 4*(4). http://www.learningcircuits.org/2003/apr2003/mars_venus.htm.

Nafay Kumail, S.M., and G. Chadha. (2005, April). "Finding the Client-Vendor Balance." *Chief Learning Officer Magazine.* http://www.clomedia.com/content/templates/clo_article.asp?articleid=919&zoneid=31.

Tyler, H. (2005, February 22). "Vendor Management Tips: Building Relationships." *Computerworld.* http://www.computerworld.com/action/article.do?command=viewArticleTOC&specialReportId=761&articleId=99816.

Zahn, D. (2001, September). "Five Steps in Working With Suppliers." *Training & Development, 55*(9): 52–55.

➤ 7

Lies About Managing the Learning Function

Edward A. Trolley

"Woe is me! They keep telling me to cut my costs and reduce my head-count, but they are telling their people not to take any of the training that we offer. I don't know what else to do. Clearly no one at my company values training, and I am not even sure if anyone values me."

Liar, liar, pants on fire! If you are an average company, you are investing $1,000 per employee per year (Sugrue, 2005) in direct spending on training and another $4,000 per employee per year in indirect spending (training-related spending associated with time off the job, travel for training, lost opportunity cost, and cost of poor quality). That hardly sounds as if no one values training, does it?

Sadly, however, this is what I hear from many training leaders. At a recent conference of chief learning officers (CLOs), it was unanimous. They were all in the same boat: budgets being cut, staff being reduced, support eroding, and their business clients not valuing what they do. What was their conclusion? The answer, they thought, was to stick together as training professionals because businesspeople just don't grasp the importance of training. The CLOs said nothing about being more client focused or creating better linkages with the business. Instead, they plotted strategies about how to weather the storm.

So, what's going on here? It's pretty clear that it's not about training; it's about results. Many training leaders are facing the same challenges:

how to be more relevant, how to be more efficient, and how to deliver the kind of value that can justify investments in training. I haven't met a businessperson yet who won't invest in something that yields measurable results and delivers real value. But, when I see training leaders conclude that business leaders don't value training because they order budget reductions, I say to them "Unless you fix the value side of the investment/value equation for training, you are on the path to going out of business." Cost is an issue to businesspeople only in the absence of value, and if value is absent, they can't make budget cuts fast enough or deep enough. Training organizations that aren't managed well may, eventually, not require any management at all.

In this chapter, you'll read about some lies about managing the learning function. Let's begin at the beginning.

Lie #1: Managing Training Is Neither Complicated nor All That Important—Anyone Can Do It.

Business executive: "We really don't have anything for Juan to do. He certainly isn't one of our top performers, and he's been through about four jobs in the past few years. Perhaps we should just bite the bullet and let him go. Wait a second. Don't we have an opening for someone in the corporate training organization? Juan doesn't know anything about it, but how hard can it be? Besides, it's not that important a job, anyway!"

For some reason, companies big and small traditionally have considered training a dumping ground for poor performers, employees who aren't really needed or wanted anywhere else, and those who at one time or another have either developed or delivered some sort of training program (or at least a set of slides) and are now considered trainers. I don't mean to demean employees who followed an untraditional path to a career in training, but given a choice you probably wouldn't put someone with a psychology degree in a chemical engineering role. Training is just like any other profession; for it to deliver the kind of value people expect of it, it has to be staffed with professionals who understand things like how adults learn, how to design a training program that will work, how to bring domain expertise into a business discussion, how to define competencies and develop curricula, and how to ensure that training is relevant and delivers measurable, meaningful business value. When you think about the investments that are being made and the business critical nature of people development, why would anyone not staff this activity for success?

Just to be clear, there are roles in a training organization that require deep domain expertise. There are also roles that require business, operations, technology, and leadership expertise and capability. This is not a one-size-fits-all situation, the same way that roles in other organizations are not. The role of CLO, or the head of training, requires someone with a very strong business sense, excellent leadership capabilities, the ability to work effectively with and have the respect of senior business executives, an understanding of how to balance fixed and variable resources, the ability to manage vendors and budgets, and finally, the ability to create confidence in customers. Of course, CLOs must know enough about the domain of training to provide leadership and guidance to the domain experts who work for them.

All training professionals need a sharper business edge than many of those who serve in training roles today. The CLO must have the sharpest edge of all.

Lie #2: Everything Is Under Control.

Business executive: "Do you have the information you need to deal with all of our issues? Is your organization as efficient and effective as it needs to be? Are you taking appropriate advantage of technology? Are you using the right processes?"

CLO: "Yes, we are in great shape. I know just what I need to know and exactly what I need to do with my organization to support the company. We are running like a smoothly oiled machine! Everything is under control."

Oh, sure! Consider this chapter to be a little test to see just how in control you are. How many of the questions posed in the sections that follow can you answer with certainty? If you don't know the answer to a question, do you know whom you would have to talk to and what data you would need to collect to get an answer to the question?

As a professional in the learning business, there are many questions you should have answers to, depending on where you sit in the training supply chain. These questions are scattered throughout this chapter.

What Is Your Company's Total Training Spend?

I don't just mean how much is in your corporate training budget. Count it all, the direct and indirect expenses. Do you have responsibility for sales training? No? Well, how much is being spent on that? What about service technicians? Are they trained in labs full of the products your company sells and plenty of test equipment? Do any business units contract directly with outside training providers? How much are they spending? How many training vendor invoices do you pay in a year? How much does it cost to pay each invoice? How much time are your employees spending off the job to attend training? Do you have any idea what their time is worth or even know how to figure this out? What about the opportunity costs that are incurred when they are away from their jobs for training? After this barrage of questions, are you still feeling in control?

Astonishingly enough, most executives—business and training—cannot answer these questions. Training is a huge investment for most companies—an average of $5,000 per employee per year (direct and indirect expenditures), and today, despite all the rhetoric on this topic, answers to these questions continue to be elusive.

Why is that a problem? If your company is really spending $100 million on training but only managing $20 million, that leaves $80 million of unmanaged spend. Any CEO probably would agree that this is a problem. Unmanaged spending on training is pervasive in many organizations, much of it occurring in business units, not in the corporate training function. Training continues to be the last of the large unmanaged expenses inside corporations, and it is imperative that learning professionals get this investment under control now or someone else will.

Are You Making a Difference Because of the Work You Do?

On a scale of 1–7, with 7 being "nailing it," how would you rate the effectiveness of your organization? Feeling pretty good about this one? Think you are a 6? What if we asked your customers? What would they say? Would they even know what you do, let alone whether it has an impact?

Training organizations usually rate themselves highly and say that their customers would agree. Yet, when I ask customers to rate the value of training, the results are often quite different. Why the discrepancy?

For one thing, customers aren't often asked this question. Learning professionals assume that because they are proud of their work and people seem to like the products and services they deliver, they are adding value to the business. Earlier in my career I reviewed the satisfaction ratings for some training programs that were offered at my company. It turned out that the highest rated courses were delivered in Florida in January! I wanted to believe that we were measuring business value, but I don't think this was the case.

Training organizations achieve credibility by consistently delivering solutions that are perceived by customers as adding value. To do that, measurement processes must identify expectations, success metrics, and influencing factors before any money is spent. Expectations and value metrics must be tracked to a conclusion. When the results are discussed with the customer and the customer agrees that the work delivered value, then, and only then, can high ratings be given. When these successes are repeated enough times that customers are assured that they will consistently get business value when they invest, the heavy-duty measurement can be replaced with a customer feedback process that confirms their satisfaction.

What Expectations Do Your Customers Have of You and Your Organization?

It is critically important to understand what your customers expect of you. Training professionals often do not know what their customers expect, and frequently they never even ask.

There is a great deal of common ground when it comes to senior executives' expectations of training organizations. During assessment activities, senior executives often indicate they expect the training function to be a business partner, to make certain that training is relevant, and that the work has measurable value. If you haven't asked, your executives haven't had the opportunity to think about the question and, therefore, you haven't had the opportunity to present yourself as a business partner. The other valuable aspect of engaging executives in this conversation is that it gives a basis for measuring your performance over time. Because high-level expectations don't typically change from year to year, measuring allows you to determine if you are improving.

Are You Adequately Leveraging Training Activities, Processes, and Technologies?

The interesting thing about training is that, not unlike other parts of the business, there are many elements of the service delivery model that can be leveraged. This means that you should be delivering some training services in one way and in one place and then applying what you do across your enterprise. You (or someone else) might say, "But we are a highly decentralized company, and we don't like centralization." Decentralized or not, your organization is still a business, and businesses don't benefit from waste, redundancy, duplication, or a lack of consistency.

You can leverage such things as learning technology, administration, vendor management, and common enterprise training needs without contradicting a decentralized business model. Being able to provide these capabilities and services one way from one place versus letting everyone "roll their own" reduces costs and improves quality, responsiveness, and consistency. Even in the most decentralized businesses, someone still worries about each of these variables.

Training organizations should take a careful look at how these technologies and services are delivered and make the business case for, at a minimum, providing them from a single source or, even more dramatically, outsourcing them when you can get further value by sharing a training infrastructure across a multicompany base.

How Are Your Training Professionals Spending Their Time?

Many organizations deploy most of their resources and dollars on low-value-add activities and underinvest in activities with high value add (van Adelsberg & Trolley, 1999). Value add for these purposes is defined as difference-making for the business.

Figure 7-1, called the camel chart because of the little hump in the middle, shows a common situation in many companies. The vertical axis is value add, and the horizontal axis is the value chain of training. As you can see, some parts of the value chain are high value add, other parts are low value add, and some parts are in between. The bars show where organizations invest their resources and dollars, and, as is evident, they are applied mostly to low-value-add, transactional activities. If you performed a detailed time study of your training professionals, you might be surprised to learn that they spend between 30 and 50 percent of their time on activities perceived by their clients as adding little value. Such a waste!

Are You as Efficient and Effective as You Can Be?

Are your costs at acceptable levels, given the value your customers are realizing? Have you uncovered, and are you managing, all of the hidden costs of training? Are you eliminating redundancies and inconsistencies and improving quality and reducing rework? Are you ensuring

Figure 7-1. The camel chart.

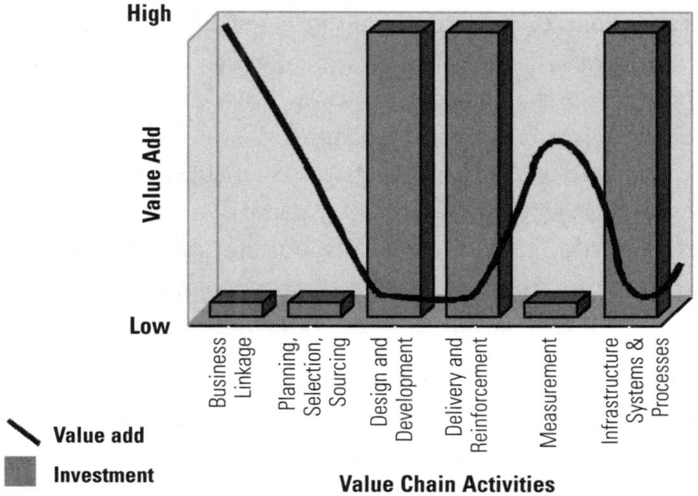

Source: Reprinted with permission of the publisher. From *Running Training Like a Business* (1999) by D. van Adelsberg and E.A. Trolley, Berrett-Koehler Publishers, San Francisco. All rights reserved.

that you understand the ways in which your customers will be evaluating your effectiveness before you begin your work? Are you using the right mix of internal and external resources so that you bring to bear as much experience and as many insights as you can? Are your fixed costs too high? Are you able to flex your resources as customer demand shifts? Are you making a difference? Is an investment in training as good an investment (if not better) as one in new equipment, new facilities, manufacturing, or research and development?

These are tough questions and ones that training organizations must be able to answer. If you don't know the answers, you sure better get them because if these questions are not being asked today, you can bet they will be in the future. And, if you can't answer them, someone else will. Self-preservation is the name of the game, folks.

By the Way, What Is the Quantifiable Value of the Work You Do?

This might just be the toughest question of all, but the training function must develop an answer. It must have processes in place to ensure that training work is relevant, connected to business needs, and able to deliver value. It's not easy; sometimes it's smoke and mirrors; sometimes your customers may even say to you "Oh, don't worry about measuring." But, this is where the rubber meets the road. Evaluation makes it possible for training leaders to stand tall with other business leaders and say that they and their organizations truly are making the kind of difference that warrants continued investment.

Training measurement is a hot topic. There are many evaluation models and many evaluation experts in the field, but the magic happens when you get pragmatic. Think about it in the same way that businesspeople think about it. Understand that there are multiple customers of training, that each of these customers has needs and expectations, and that each customer's needs are unique. Find out what their

Evaluation makes it possible for training leaders to stand tall with other business leaders and say that they and their organizations truly are making the kind of difference that warrants continued investment.

needs are and how they measure success; then make certain that the training solutions, whatever they might be, move the levers on each and every one of these metrics.

It is problematic if even one of the seven questions above cannot be answered with certainty, but my sense is that the number is a lot higher than one for most organizations. Training should be run like a business (sound familiar?) and, in that regard, it is essential that you understand how much you are spending, what you are spending it on, how you are delivering your products and services, and how your customers derive value from it. That's not too much to ask, is it? Every other part of the business is held to these standards. So, why not training?

How do you get answers to all of these questions and more? I suggest a process called a training assessment or—even better—a strategic training assessment. I am not talking about a needs analysis here, but instead, a complete, end-to-end assessment of all training activities inside the company with the objective of understanding the current and future states of training (table 7-1).

Table 7-1. Conducting a strategic training assessment.

The Current State of Training	The Required Future State of Training
• How much is being spent?	• How much should be spent?
• What is it being spent on?	• What should it be spent on?
• What processes and technology are used to support and deliver services?	• What processes and technologies should be in place to support and deliver the services?
• What is the quality of the training products and services?	• How should the training be built and delivered?
• What are the capabilities of current training professionals and how are they being deployed?	• What types of training professionals are required and how should they be deployed?
• How well are customer expectations being met and the results being realized?	• What are customers' expectations?
	• What key business drivers must training support?
	• How will training activity be governed?

If you manage to grasp an understanding of all these topics and questions, you will be much better equipped to evaluate and assess the effectiveness of your training.

Huge opportunities exist to improve the effectiveness and efficiency of training in most, if not all, organizations. To make these improvements, it is critical that a thorough understanding of the current state of training be developed. In line with that old saying: "If you don't know where you are going, any road will take you there," it is essential that training leaders understand clearly the future state requirements of their products and services and have a strategy and action plan to close the gap between the two.

Can you do this work yourself? Sure, but you would be better served by an outside organization whose core competence is conducting this type of analysis. The work will be more targeted, better focused, and more comprehensive, and, at the same time, you will gain valuable insights from the data they have collected from companies that previously participated in this type of analysis.

The truth is that learning professionals are rarely in control. In fact, even if equipped with answers to all of these questions, professionals still wouldn't really be in control because most of the data would be out of date as soon as it's collected and interpreted. However, knowing the difference between what you know and what you don't know puts you in a much better position to collect the information you need to make better—if not perfect—decisions that support the needs of your customers. In the end, you can only try to control the things you can control and learn to work around the rest.

Lie #3: Size Matters.

Josh Bersin (2005) says, "In the traditional corporate university model, developed over the last 30 years, companies create a 'place to go' to learn. These organizations have many offerings to choose from, they are centralized and located at corporate headquarters, and are staffed for peak demand."

Corporate universities aren't alone in taking this approach. Remember the days of large training organizations with large staffs of trainers? This was common practice in the not-too-distant past and, in

Knowing the difference between what you know and what you don't know puts you in a much better position to collect the information you need to make better—if not perfect—decisions that support the needs of your customers.

fact, some organizations today still believe big is good. What is needed is a different model that keeps fixed costs down and leverages variable resources and costs to provide the training services required of their customers. Training has characteristics that don't support high fixed costs. A detailed discussion of a few of these characteristics is the focus of the next few sections.

The Cyclical Nature of Training
Where do you draw the line on fixed costs so that you do not have excess staff when demand for training is down, but you do not pay excessive and premium fees when need exceeds capacity?

One approach to minimize fixed costs is to respond to periodic increased needs with variable resources. This is important because business managers don't like fixed costs that are allocated to them regardless of whether they use the associated services. Business managers expect you to manage costs in a way that enables them to pay for most of what they get when they use it. Large training organizations must cover their costs. Even those that claim to have charge-back systems that bill out all of their costs are naïve in that there are always times when costs exceed demand; the costs must go somewhere—usually to the businesses through some sort of allocation scheme. Training leaders who run departments with high fixed costs are walking around with a "kick me" sign on their backs, setting themselves up to be kicked by businesspeople who dislike fixed costs (van Adelsberg & Trolley, 1999).

Training Is Primarily Discretionary
Unfortunately for large training organizations, training costs are widely considered to be discretionary and, therefore, subject to budget reductions or even complete elimination. Fixed costs continue even if training

resources are not being utilized, so when there is not much training to do, resources sit idly, and that is waste.

Training Benefits From an Outside Perspective

Organizations that look primarily to internal resources for their training solutions are missing a huge opportunity to tap into the expertise and experience that third-party providers gain from having worked with other companies. Some argue that outside providers are too expensive and that training organizations can keep their costs down by using internal resources to do the work. This decision, however, must be supported with a business case. For example:

➤ Are fixed costs better than variable costs?
➤ Do internal resources have the breadth of experience and expertise to bring world-class training solutions to your customers?
➤ Do you know how other companies have responded to these types of business needs?
➤ Are your internal resources fully utilized or are you incurring down-time costs that you wouldn't have with external resources?

I have seen several very large training organizations dramatically reduce the number of training people they have on staff. These companies didn't stop training. They just changed their fixed cost model to one that utilized variable resources and variable costs.

So, this is not really a lie. Size does matter in training, and small is good!

Lie #4: It's All About the Numbers.

Training staffer: "Look at the charts. All the numbers are up: the number of titles we offer, the number of sessions we deliver, the number of people we train, the number of vendors we use, the amount of money we spend, the number of training resources we control."

That's great, right? Wrong! Many years ago when I was the new head of training for a very large company, this was the response from my staff when I asked them what value they were adding to the business.

Unfortunately, they confused internal training volume metrics with the value metrics of our customers.

Although volume and activity levels are important to measure and they certainly need to be managed, they are not important without the context of value. If all the numbers are up except for value, then there is a serious problem. And, that problem will eventually lead to a dramatic action. The value of training must be reflected in numbers, in measures such as increased revenue, improved productivity, reduced manufacturing costs, improved customer retention, and other important business measures in addition to the volume and activity measures. Those business measures are the ones that answer the question, "What value is training adding?"

Lie #5: It's a Function—Behave Like One.

Accounting department staffer: "Training, ugh, you're a support function, you're overhead, you're not part of the business, you're a cost center, you don't add value to the business, you're a burden to our business."

If you have spent any time in human resources (HR), finance, accounting, or purchasing, you have likely heard your organization described using one or more of the phrases above or others not as kind. Actually, back in the day, data processing before it became information technology, or IT, was a charter member of this group. It was characterized by high costs, its people talked a different language, success was measured in kbps, bps, memory, number of computers, number of programs. To top off its bad reputation, the people in data processing walked around with geeky haircuts and pocket protectors; they could not explain to other departments what they really did, day in and day out.

Today, those same people are wearing Armani suits, being called chief information officers, and sitting at the executive table. If you are wondering how that happened, here's the story: In the mid-1980s, data processors, faced with the same challenges training is facing today (cost pressure, headcount reductions, and challenges from business regarding the value being received from the investment) chose to transform themselves from technologists to businesspeople. In so doing, they began talking about how their technologies could be used to achieve competitive advantage and started demonstrating that their work was critical to the success of the business. Most important, they became businesspeople in IT, not IT people in business.

The path is clear for training. Table 7-2 lists a set of transformations that must take place for training to move from the backroom to the boardroom.

To take this a step further, you should consider creating annual business plans and annual reports, just like your customers do. Some organizations, including Caterpillar and Defense Acquisition University, excel at producing such reports. (These two companies have been recognized as best in class by Corporate University Exchange and *Chief Learning Officer Magazine*. You would be well served to benchmark them.)

There is never a better time than now to begin the transformation. Following the IT path will lead to the pot of gold at the end of the rainbow, and you will be recognized rightfully as businesspeople who are in training, and your organization will move from a functional orientation to a business enterprise orientation.

Table 7-2. Training transformations.

From:	To:
Training department	Training enterprise
Cost of training	Investment in learning
Attendees	Customers
Measuring activity levels	Measuring results
What training do you need?	What business issue are you trying to solve?
Training as the end result	Business results as the end result
Mastering content	Improving performance
Allocation of expense	Pay for use
Activity	Application
Smile sheets	Customer success

Lie #6: There's No Burning Platform.

Head of corporate training: "We have 50 training organizations in our company with 50 training managers, multiple learning management systems, hundreds of training vendors, and we don't know how much we are spending or what we are getting for the spending. But, my chief executive officer believes in training and doesn't care what we spend. There's no burning platform to force any of us to do anything about this situation."

This was part of a conversation I had a couple of years ago with one of the 50 heads of training in this organization. She really did believe that her chief executive officer (CEO) didn't care how much money was being spent. My parting words to her as I left the meeting were, "Someday, sometime, you are going to get a call from either the chief financial officer (CFO) or the CEO telling you that the party is over and that unmanaged, uncontrolled spending is not acceptable. They may just shut you down."

The issue here is not that there was no burning platform but that this group of training leaders didn't understand that there was. If this training head and the other 49 training heads had a business orientation, they would not be waiting for someone to tell them that something has to be done. They would take the initiative to address these issues of high fixed costs, waste, redundancy, and unmanaged spending. They would figure out that there should be one technology platform serving the enterprise and that understanding how much is being spent is critical. They would be leveraging activities and services that should be done one way in one place. If they failed to fix these situations, eventually someone would take the action for them, burning the platform right out from under them.

Lie #7: Do It Myself = GOOD!
Outsource = BAD! (or Vice Versa).

CLO to training outsourcing provider: "There's just no way that your company can run training for my organization. You are not in our industry, and you don't know our business. That's why outsourcing is not a good option for us. Besides, outsourcing doesn't work."

There are a number of lies specifically related to outsourcing, from both the buyer and provider sides. Therefore, Lie #7 will be broken down into a number of "sub-lies" so that it can be addressed adequately.

Sub-Lie #1: Outsourcing Reduces Costs.
Outsourcing Doesn't Reduce Costs.

Depending on whom you talk to, you could hear either one of these blanket statements regarding outsourcing. It is amazing that this debate continues. Perhaps it's not a debate but, instead, at least from the training-leader side of the aisle, more of a smokescreen. Outsourcing across various functions like IT, HR, finance, and accounting can achieve cost reductions, if that is what the client wants out of the relationship.

Consider the example of HR. HR outsourcers are confident in their ability to reduce costs because the work they take on is mostly, if not completely, transactional. (HR is estimated to be 70 percent transactional and 30 percent strategic.) Benefits of outsourcing result from leveraging scale, common processes, and technologies. The picture gets even better if the outsourcer can provide services to its clients in a variable cost model so that the client does not have to carry high fixed costs and can pay for the services as they are used on a per-transaction basis. The research reports and case studies on this are quite consistent: Outsourcing can deliver cost reductions.

Training, however, is different. Unlike HR's transaction-heavy activities, the majority of training's value chain activities are strategic, not transactional, and, unlike payroll, benefits, and other HR services, training activities are largely discretionary. Therefore, if cost reduction is the key driver, you can just reduce the amount of training you offer or stop it completely. Not surprisingly, your costs will drop dramatically. The central issue with training is the broken investment/value equation, so any training outsourcing activity must be ultimately driven by the need to increase value. Training outsourcers, particularly those who take on the transactional elements of training such as technology, administration, and vendor management, can reduce the costs of these activities. But so what? If you reduce by 30 percent a line item that only comprises 30 percent of the total spend, you would save less than 10 percent of the entire cost. If you don't fix the value side of the equation, then business leaders will continue to say that training still costs too much and your outsourcing strategy will fail.

So back to the sub-lie: Does training outsourcing reduce costs or doesn't it? Outsourcing is most likely to save money in transactional areas but increase costs in more strategic areas. Overall, you should look for a reduction in the unit cost of training (costs per person per day/hour/year). That is the true measure of efficiency for training as it means redundancy has been eliminated, the quality of processes has improved, technology and other resources are being leveraged, hidden costs are exposed and being managed, and people are being deployed in such a way that value add is increasing. When the value of training dramatically improves, training will be deemed an excellent investment, and companies will spend more, not less, on this valued function.

Sub-Lie #2: No One Knows My Business as I Do.

This is another one of those smokescreens put forth by internal training resources. Outsourcing does not mean that you stop accessing the subject matter expertise of your business clients. It does mean that you begin accessing resources and capabilities that are professional, skilled, trained, experienced, and best in class in doing what they do.

Companies have been outsourcing or out-tasking (having an outside provider perform a finite task such as delivering a training program) various parts of the training function forever, particularly to gain access to content. That is why there is such a huge market for training companies. These training companies work with their customers, both training resources and subject matter experts, to put together learning solutions that solve business needs. These training companies understand how to design, develop, and deliver training, and they apply those capabilities to the subject matter or business need at hand. Even the folks who say, "No outsider can know my business like I do," tap into these providers for help from time to time.

Training outsourcers bring the same capabilities and more. Not only do they have access to training expertise, but they also understand processes, operations, and technology. They bring all of these together in an integrated way to serve their customers. In all probability, the only thing that is truly proprietary in your business is the subject matter, and even training resources have to draw on the expertise of their business partners to develop effective learning solutions. All the surrounding training processes, including design, development, delivery, technology, administration, vendor management, and others, are fairly generic and certainly aren't compromised by the outsourcing provider not knowing your business as you do.

Sub-Lie #3: It Is Taboo to Outsource Strategic Training Activities.

This is a myth perpetuated by both training leaders and training outsourcers who don't offer the services and, therefore, argue that strategic services should not be outsourced. The most strategic of training activities is the process of understanding the direction, strategy, challenges, issues, objectives, and goals of the business and then identifying ways in which training can add value. This is the beginning of the beginning. If this isn't done right, nothing else matters.

Several years ago, I did a training outsourcing deal where the customer said that it had to retain the relationship management role, so we set up the operational process in a way that the customer's training resources would work with the businesses to determine the needs and then work with us to deliver solutions. Within a very short time, the head of training for this company received calls from almost all of the senior business leaders asking: "What's new about this? These are the same people who have not served my business well in the past. You promised me transformation with this outsourcing initiative, not more of the same!" Suffice it to say, the training leader acted quickly and moved the relationship management role to the outsourcing partner. We brought in people who had extensive experience doing exactly this type of work. Their compensation was based on how well they understood their customers' needs and how effective their solutions had been in delivering business value. The head of training made the right decision by outsourcing the relationship management role, and the business benefited.

Some people call this activity performance consulting or training consulting. I prefer relationship management, a business term that businesspeople understand. Relationship managers understand their customers' business, live inside the business, sit at the business table, look for ways to make a difference, and bring broad business insights to their customers. These are the businesspeople within training. They understand business, and they know when training can help and when it cannot. They don't ask businesspeople, "What training do you need?" Instead, they talk about what the sales or market share or productivity improvement objectives are and present specific ways by which training (or related products and services) can help to achieve them.

It is understandable why internal training resources might argue against outsourcing the relationship-management part of the training value chain. What is not clear is why so many training outsourcers agree. I think there are two major reasons:

➤ They see their business as transactional, not transformational. Therefore, they don't have a service offering that extends across the entire value chain of training, but, instead, focuses solely on the transactional elements.

➤ They don't want to create conflict with a potential client for fear of losing their chance at the transactional opportunity. The client is always right, right?

Buyer beware! If your providers always agree with you, then you are not getting the kind of insight, expertise, and know-how that you deserve and are paying for.

Sub-Lie #4: People Don't Lose Their Jobs When You Outsource.

In the past year, I have been on numerous panels with outsourcing providers who say that training resources don't lose their jobs in an outsourcing deal. My response always is that providers need to stop sugarcoating this. The entry ticket for training outsourcing is cost reduction. Sixty-seven percent of respondents in the *2005 ASTD State of the Industry Report* (Sugrue, 2005) said that the decision to outsource was driven primarily by a need to reduce operating costs.

It is impossible to take out the necessary costs without eliminating jobs. Outsourcers who promise no job losses are simply not telling the truth. They can't deliver on that promise and deliver the results you are expecting. So it isn't a question of whether job losses will occur, only when they will occur. By the way, if your goal is to reduce costs and you don't outsource, there may still be job losses, only the numbers may be higher.

So why do outsourcers continue to make these statements? It's back to the conflict issue. Training outsourcers say what you want to hear so that they don't jeopardize their opportunity with you. Again, buyer beware!

Sub-Lie #5: If I Outsource, I Will Lose Control.

This is the biggest lie of all. In many organizations, training continues to be one of the largest unmanaged expenses. Training is pervasive—it happens everywhere. Most of the spend, in fact, occurs outside of the official corporate training function. There are multiple systems and processes and many people engaged in the design, development, and delivery of training. Very few organizations know how much they spend in total, and, consequently, there is little control over the investment. It is difficult to ensure that there is no waste, redundancy, or inconsistency and that quality and value measures are consistent. It's not as if you were actually in control to begin with.

Now, enter outsourcing. If you choose to outsource in a comprehensive way, you will work with a partner to figure out how much is being spent; where it is being spent; what processes, technology, and people are being utilized; where duplication and redundancy exist; and so on. When your partner works with you to get all of the above under one roof and transformed and then has responsibility for management of the whole thing, your company will finally have a single point of accountability with service-level agreements and management of costs and quality. Then, finally, you will actually be in control.

I have seen control increase dramatically through the outsourcing process and that holds true for whatever the scope of the outsourcing arrangement is. Being able to look to one provider for all of the accountability, metrics, responsibility, and costs is a value add for the outsourcing decision.

Lie #8: It's About Training.

This is the mother of all lies. I began this chapter with a short story about training leaders finding themselves in a situation where their bosses are telling them to cut headcount and costs and their response is, "Woe is me!" It is disheartening that in 2006, too many training leaders think that it's about training. Training is important, competencies must be built, training is good, and training is a demonstration of how a company values its people. Although all those things are true, it's really not about training—it's about results. Those assertions must be put in the context of some business imperative. For example, these statements reframe the value of training from a business leader's perspective:

> ➤ "Training is important because it builds the selling skills of our sales organization so that they can meet our growth objectives of a 15 percent increase in revenue."
> ➤ "Training is valuable because we have evidence that investments in our employees lead to increased retention, which, in turn, results in higher retention of customers."

At the end of the day, executives have to make decisions about how they invest their company's (and shareholders') money. Those decisions involve options that compete for investments based on the value they will deliver to the business. Training must deliver tangible value. The days of training's feel-good charter are over. Training is now in the business realm, where it must deliver value and it must be willing to be held to the same accountabilities and business metrics as other investments.

That means that managing the training function is really now about running the training function like a business. Training must move from its functional orientation to a business orientation. It must be effective and efficient; it must be customer driven, results focused, and value producing. The people in the training organization must be businesspeople within training, understanding that their work must make a difference, that they must understand the business of their customers, and that their success is measured by the success of their customers.

How to Take Your Training Function to the Next Level

There are key points to keep in mind if you are considering improving the overall management of your learning function. To do this, you should have answers to the following questions:

- ➤ Are you as efficient as you need to be?
- ➤ Have you eliminated waste and redundancy, improved quality, and reduced rework?
- ➤ Are you leveraging people, processes, and technology appropriately?
- ➤ Have you uncovered and are you managing all the hidden costs?
- ➤ Do you have the right mix of fixed and variable resources and spend?
- ➤ Are you utilizing outsourcing as a tool to improve efficiency and gain scalability?
- ➤ Are you as effective as you need to be?
- ➤ Is the work you do relevant to the business?
- ➤ Are you tightly linked to the needs of the business?
- ➤ Do you know if you are meeting your customers' expectations?
- ➤ Have you quantified the value of your work?
- ➤ Are you accessing outside expertise at an appropriate level?

If you don't have answers to these questions, perhaps you should consider a comprehensive and strategic assessment of your learning activities. If you do, look to the outside for help on this. The benefits will far exceed the investment.

Do you have a process for ensuring senior business leader engagement, involvement, and support of the work you do? A strong, formal governance process is crucial to success. Get it started now.

Move from a functional orientation to a business orientation. Change the way you think and talk. Install business processes and a service delivery model that engages customers, uncovers business needs, provides high-quality solution options, and ensures that your solution delivery is impeccable. Then, measure what matters.

Is outsourcing a viable option for you to consider? Outsourcing comes in various flavors; it is not an all-or-nothing proposition. You owe it to your business, to yourself, and to your organization to be open to this option for improving effectiveness and efficiency. Try it; you might like it!

Overcoming the Lies With Truth

In this chapter, I have addressed some of the lies about managing the learning function and discussed some of the misconceptions about outsourcing, the need to focus on both efficiency and effectiveness, how to gain control over the activity, and how learning professionals have to think about managing the training function as if it's a business.

The work you do must always be considered in the context of supporting a business need. Learning professionals must justify themselves by the value they deliver to the business, not by volume and activity levels. Therefore, measures must relate to the business of training and the work of training. Customer retention, cycle time, quality, costs, and the extent to which customers' expectations are met are as important as the first three levels of Donald Kirkpatrick's (1998) evaluation model. The most important measure is the business value your customer receives from his or her investment in you. That is what businesses worry about and that is what training should worry about. Your success, as with any business, should be measured by the success of your customers.

The questions, steps, and self-assessments that were provided in this chapter can help you decide if you are prepared to take your company to the next level. If you find you are indeed prepared, they should give you a place to start.

And, always remember: It's not about training.

The Lie	The Truth
Managing training is neither complicated nor all that important—anyone can do it.	Training is just like any other profession; for it to deliver the kind of value people expect of it, it has to be staffed with professionals who understand things like how adults learn, how to design a training program that will work, how to bring domain expertise into a business discussion, how to define competencies and develop curricula, and how to ensure that training is relevant and delivers measurable, meaningful business value.
Everything is under control.	Learning professionals are rarely under control. However, knowing the difference between what you know and what you don't know puts you in a much better position to collect the information you need to make better—if not perfect—decisions that support the needs of your customers.
Size matters.	Some organizations today still believe big is good, but what is needed is a different model that keeps fixed costs down and leverages variable resources and costs to provide the training services required of their customers. Training has characteristics that don't support high fixed costs.
It's all about the numbers.	Although volume and activity levels are important to measure and they certainly need to be managed, they are not important without the context of value. The value of training must be reflected in measures such as increased revenue, improved productivity, reduced manufacturing costs, improved customer retention, and other important business measures in addition to the volume and activity measures.
It's a function—behave like one.	Your organization can move from a functional orientation to a business enterprise orientation. To do so, training must embark on a set of transformations to move from the backroom to the boardroom.
There's no burning platform.	The party is over. Unmanaged, uncontrolled spending by training is not acceptable. Eventually someone in the organization will take the initiative to address issues of high fixed costs, waste, redundancy, and unmanaged spending, burning the platform right out from under the training function.
Do it myself = GOOD! Outsource = BAD! (or vice versa).	Outsourcing comes in various flavors; it is not an all-or-nothing proposition. You owe it to your business, to yourself, and to your organization to be open to this option for improving effectiveness and efficiency.
It's about training.	Training is important, competencies must be built, training is good, and training is a demonstration of how a company values its people. Although all those things are true, it's really not about training—it's about results.

References

Bersin, J. (2005, November). "Death of Corporate Universities, Birth of Learning Services." Oakland, CA: Bersin & Associates. http://www.bersin.com/tips_techniques/05_nov_death_cu.asp.

Kirkpatrick, D. (1998). *Evaluating Training Programs: The Four Levels* (2nd edition). San Francisco: Berrett-Koehler.

Sugrue, B. (2005). *2005 State of the Industry Report.* Alexandria, VA: ASTD Press.

van Adelsberg, D., and E.A. Trolley. (1999). *Running Training Like a Business.* San Francisco: Berrett-Koehler.

Lies About E-Learning

Elliott Masie

Adding the letter "e" in front of any term triggers an avalanche of lies. For example: Email has made our organization so much more productive, or e-commerce will be the end of stores. The letter "e" brings a dot.com hyper-enthusiasm and hyper-cynicism to any process. The marketplace starts to lie to itself, as well as to investors and customers about the readiness and economic model of the new phenomena. The change-resistant adopter lies about how it will never work. The sentimentalist weaves lies about the effectiveness and efficiency of the good old days, and the futurist lies to audiences about how things will never be the same again. (I can plead guilty to that one on multiple counts!)

Lies about e-learning follow this pattern perfectly. They are reflective of both the optimism and naïveté of the learning field. They have enabled large-scale experiments and implementations of new learning approaches on a worldwide basis. They have moved the active phrase in our field from training to learning. They have rapidly pushed early investments in learning management systems (LMSs). And, they have triggered an enterprisewide view of learning.

Thus, you see my perspective on lies about e-learning. Most are unintentional. Some have been downright helpful. I even confess to promulgating a few of them myself, being an early advocate of e-learning.

Nevertheless, this chapter is not a confessional. I'm going to examine a few of the key lies to help create the next chapter of learning with greater wisdom and reality.

Lie #1: E-Learning Is New.

Nope, e-learning has been around for a very long time. It started long before Al Gore or whoever invented the Internet. When Admiral Grace Hopper, the godmother of mainframe computing, saw her first system go live in 1944, she predicted that these new machines called computers would someday help teach sailors how to do their jobs. But, e-learning started earlier than that when the advent of commercial radio in the 1920s was accompanied by early experiments in delivering classroom lessons to the children of farmers in rural areas.

> When I was 7 years old in P.S. 173 in New York City, we did e-learning every week. Mrs. Ham took us into a classroom and, as the audiovisual monitor, I loaded up a filmstrip into the projector, dimmed the lights, and created an e-learning experience (or a short nap time) for my fellow second graders.

Certainly, the concept of e-learning derived from computer-based training (CBT). Structured and branched classes were designed and delivered first on mainframe computers and later on stand-alone personal computers and video disks. Next, CBT entered the network arena when shared courses started to be mounted on organizations' F drives. Finally, with the advent of the Internet, the phrase "e-learning" was introduced.

I can guess I was one of the first analysts and writers to start using the term e-learning. In the early 1990s, I used it as a prediction of the educational use of email and networks such as CompuServe. The key point is that e-learning was not an invention of the Internet. It has rich and important roots in decades of experimentation and deployment of technology to help create, deliver, inspire, and assess learning. Clearly, e-learning is also a derivative of the educational and pedagogical approaches of theorists including Dewey, Skinner, and Gagne.

The key point is that e-learning was not an invention of the Internet. It has rich and important roots in decades of experimentation and deployment of technology to help create, deliver, inspire, and assess learning.

This lie is important because too much of the dialog about e-learning has been with a historical basis. Deep research and practice about how learners process information, how competencies can be assessed, and how curriculum can be designed effectively are embedded in this lie. When the dot.com era hit, many folks jumped onto the e-learning bandwagon without any context or history. In fact, some of the lies of earlier learning technology rollouts were unknowingly repeated:

➤ Educational television will make the classroom obsolete.
➤ Overhead projectors will add excitement to the delivery of instruction.
➤ Computer-based instruction will dramatically lower the cost of training employees.

E-learning is a powerful and evolving set of tools and strategies. But, e-learning has a history and a set of forgotten historical perspectives. The future of e-learning cannot be invented if the past of e-learning is not acknowledged and taken into account.

Lie #2: E-Learning Works!

This is a lie because there is an acute lack of reliable research and a large dose of fuzzy thinking about the actual effectiveness of specific e-learning programs. A large percentage of e-learning is effective with the right learners in the right situations, but some e-learning is just a digital page turner that does not result in knowledge acquisition or transfer. Unfortunately, many organizations and even suppliers do not fully understand the pattern of effectiveness of e-learning.

Before determined critics of e-learning start quoting this module as ammunition against e-learning, ask yourself if this sounds familiar: Classroom instruction works! It is often impossible to tell. And, the type of research that would give us greater confidence in the true effectiveness of a specific form of instructional delivery has not been invested in.

How and When Does E-Learning Work?

The answer to this question would be a great way of starting the conversation about its relative effectiveness. This approach acknowledges the varied effectiveness of different designs, content levels, learning activities, durations, assessment intensities, and job aids. A single company or instructional designer would gather great insight into the effectiveness of e-learning for his or her situation. Yet, as a field, a mechanism for addressing the ground truth of the efficacy of varied e-learning approaches is missing.

Why Does Lie #2 Get Promulgated?

Multiple factors are involved in the perseverance of this lie. Here are several reasons:

> *Completion data is a false positive.* Large numbers of e-learning deployments measure the quantity of completions. This is increasing in the age of compliance, as organizations are turning to e-learning to create legal coverage against liability or regulator investigations. "They all took the e-learning!"

> *Often, e-learning tests only short-term memory.* E-learning provides an easy way to test for short-term memory and comprehension. You can teach a screen of information and then quickly test to see if the learner has gotten it. However, that may not convert to long-term comprehension or transfer to the workplace. Yet, the data is collectable and reportable.

> *Learning is usually blended.* Most learners don't learn from just the e-learning modules that come across their screen. They do a personalized version of blended learning. The learner absorbs information and creates his or her own practice, gets help from a peer in the workplace, or even takes a follow-up class to get across the finish line of performance. The e-learning may be a large or small piece of the formula for learner effectiveness.

➤ *The value is in the offer.* In many instances, the organization is more interested in making the visible offer of the e-learning resources, rather than clearly measuring the effectiveness of specific programs.

If someone claims that all e-learning works equally well, he or she is caught in another bold-faced lie and not one that I actually hear from the mouths of my learning colleagues. In any collection of resources, there are variations in value and effectiveness. But, I defy you to show me how the manager or learner determines the relative effectiveness of e-learning from a list of courses or offerings on an organization's learning webpage. It isn't there. Instead, learning professionals tend to homogenize the appearance and effectiveness of course offerings.

Here is what learners might find useful and valuable:

➤ *Ratings from peers:* Let the learners benefit from one another's ratings. Give them an opportunity to rate learning resources.
➤ *Ratings from experts:* Learners would greatly benefit from hearing the ratings of specific programs from experts. I still attend movies that critics have rated a B or even C+.
➤ *Presentation style information:* This part of the description would explain the type of learning experience that the module offers. The learner would like a better description of the style of the e-learning (for example, page turner, testing throughout, simulation, role play, job-aid-centric, performance support).
➤ *Learning style feedback:* Learners would benefit from instrumentation that would give them feedback on how they are most effective as learners. Help the learner understand which types of learning resources tend to be most helpful to them.

On a meta-level, it's time to invest in learning research! Several studies indicate that there is a correlation in effectiveness between classroom and online instruction, but that is not enough. An international effort to create research on the relative effectiveness and efficiency of diverse e-learning programs in diverse situations would be enormously beneficial. Too many doctoral studies are focused on university students and short-term testing. Workplace-based research on e-learning effectiveness must be funded.

Lie #3: E-Learning Is Just an Online Class.

Too much e-learning is a poor imitation of a great instructor-led class. This is predictable, as each innovation tends to use the metaphor of its predecessor. For example, early television shows were modeled after radio shows. Even classrooms were modeled after religious institutions. The lectern looks just like a church's pulpit.

Let's not be constrained by the class metaphor. So what exactly happens when you "e" classroom instruction?

> *Slow starts:* E-learning designers use the same slow start as the classroom instructor. Learning professionals build these introductory modules that are usually worthless and students often hate. Why take five minutes to teach someone how to navigate? Learn from the world of gaming, where it just starts. Teach navigation as you go and use standard templates so that students develop muscle memory and instincts for their e-learning.

> *Student language:* Stop calling the consumer a student or a learner! Why take them back to the classroom mentality? If you are deploying e-learning at work, make it feel like work. The classroom will always feel like a place away from work, but let's make e-learning look and even smell like the world of work. Don't call the expert the teacher, and don't call the consumer a student. Remember, when learners feel like students, they often display many of the dysfunctional behaviors of their earlier days in school: higher passivity and even sitting in the back of the classroom. Turn e-learning into active learning.

> *Linear instruction:* As an instructional designer, I was taught to focus on scope and sequence. Define for the learners what they will learn and give them the perfect sequence for acquiring the new skill. In an instructor-led class, designers have to make a set of sequence decisions. Yet, e-learning gives the

learner the ability to break the linear sequence. In fact, some learners thrive on learning things backward. Start at the end result and work backward. Let the learner skip to the highest interest module and navigate from there.

➤ *Dismissal bell:* A classroom model assumes that the learner will be there from the start of the lesson until the end or the bell goes off. Most e-learning is not geared toward visitation and positive departure. I want to be able to take a module and leave for a while, if I so desire, and easily come back and continue. Let's use the flexibility of the e-learning to create more comfortable access and departure.

➤ *One voice—one instructor:* A large percentage of e-learning is designed with a single voice of expertise. The instructor viewpoint is presented. Why not enlarge the voices in the room, including diverse opinions. Bring in content or even media clips of multiple folks with diverse opinions on the content. Don't be afraid of conflict, in fact use textured approaches to make e-learning more lively and engaging.

➤ *Note-taking challenges:* We are not helping e-learners with their notation needs. Learners want to be able to highlight, annotate, and add context to your notes and handouts. In classrooms, learning professionals acknowledge that learners will be marking up their well-designed notes to make them their own. Yet, in e-learning, learners are rarely given the opportunity to personalize the learning content. Learning vendors, take note. (No pun intended!)

Lie #4: E-Learning Pricing is Sensible.

Wow, now that is a lie! Professionals are at an extremely confusing point on pricing in the e-learning world. This applies to both the pricing of e-learning content as well as learning systems such as learning content management systems (LCMSs). It is not surprising because the field is changing, and there is confusion about the pricing of all digital content. Pricing is confusing for buyers and suppliers as they structure their offerings.

Equivalency Pricing

Should an e-learning course be the same price as its classroom equivalent? Clearly, the organization may save significant expenses on travel and lodging, but is the learner really getting the same services and values? Does the e-learning offering provide coaching and remediation for the confused learner? And, are you paying for delivery of content or is the price for transfer?

Content Salad Bar Pricing

How should organizations pay for access to large collections of e-learning content? In the early days of CBT, organizations purchased content on an "all-you-can-eat" salad bar model. The concept was to pay a fee for each named user that gave the user permission to take as many courses as he or she liked throughout the year. In many ways, the fee was for the "offer" rather than the delivery. However, in some organizations, the full consumption of courses did not match the value of the subscription fees, which were subsequently renegotiated.

Pay for Completion or Access

Learners are grazing e-learning. They are popping into a course and effectively consuming the one module they need. But, this approach is causing deep confusion on the pricing front. Should this type of use be charged as a completion or should organizations be paying for library access to large collections of modules?

Learning Systems Variations

There is a huge variation in the actual pricing of LMSs and LCMSs. What should an organization pay per user or per server for a full functioning LMS or LCMS? There are no guidelines or an easy answer to this logical question because of the enormous fluctuation in pricing models in the industry at this moment. The newness of the LMS marketplace and the wide range of customization requirements have made pricing a minefield for procurement groups.

Pricing for learning products and services needs a tune-up. As an industry, take a fresh look at pricing (without raising any antitrust issues):

➤ *New pricing models for learning content collections:* Loaded access, average utilization, or even total bandwidth of content consumed could be explored in content collection pricing.

➤ *Value-based pricing:* Experiment with assigning varied value to content based on impact to the organization. One might even look to analytics such as increased sales to find a linkage between content and price.

➤ *Benchmarking on pricing:* Improve industrywide surveys of pricing on specific content, systems, and services to provide a perspective on the changing marketplace.

Lie #5: E-Learning Has a Future.

This isn't really a lie, unless I am arrogantly saying that we really know the future of e-learning. There are some trends, however, based on evolutions in learning, technology, and even society at large that can inform the planning, evaluation, and purchase of learning systems, content, and services.

The Fading "E"

The "e" is a transitional term. It made great sense when the most provocative thing about e-learning was that it was electronic and delivered to the learner via the World Wide Web. But, that is not really new anymore. When I take a module or course online, it is just plain learning. As other digital phenomena have become popularized, the "e" tends to fade. I don't think of ordering a book from Amazon as e-commerce. I don't think of checking into my JetBlue flight as e-check-in; it's just a convenient time saver. The same is true for e-learning. Watch for

➤ the fading of e-learning roles and titles in corporations, such as vice presidents of learning or chief learning officers (CLOs)

➤ the leveraging of learning systems for all flavors of learning activities including online, coaching, simulations, classroom, on-the-job training, and others

➤ the rise of blended learning as a larger percentage of organizational learning and performance efforts, combining the best of digital content with alternative activities.

The Media Richness of Web and E-Learning Experiences Grows

The learning profession is moving toward the posttext stage of its web experience. In the first decade of the web, learning professionals were excited to get relevant text (with varied cool fonts and colors) and an occasional picture or graphic. Now, expectations are for a richer and fuller media experience. The rapid acceptance of iPods and MP3 players, along with the rise of video on demand, has lubricated the way for a more visual and audio set of content. Look for the following learning evolutions in the near future:

➤ *Audio everywhere:* The creation and publishing of audio is one of the easy and low-cost capacities that will shake web experiences. Telephones or PC microphones will be used to make instant knowledge and context objects, which can be linked to sites with a single click. Audio content from the CEO or a key customer will bring daily, personalized radio-type shows to computers or mobile devices.

➤ *Video bandwidth available:* Your IT departments will reluctantly enter the video era. While they fought the impacts of video on uptime and bandwidth requirements for years, the game is about to end. Organizational requirements to deliver video to customers, supply chain partners, employees, and even job prospects will hit quickly and broadly. You will be in charge of your own video-feed editing. Learners will have access to multiple perspectives, segments, and even camera views.

➤ *The resurgence of video conferencing:* Video conferencing was once a herky-jerky picture and unsure audio feed, usually limited to expensive room systems right off the chief executive officer's suite. That is about to change dramatically! Low-cost, high-quality video over the Internet will allow learners to be linked live to expertise, internally and externally, with a single click. This will supercharge your ability to offer regular access to coaching, assessment, and context-based expertise on a global basis. Watch for the first rise of video conferencing in the home to link families to their elders in assisted living facilities. Cable modem services are targeting this application as one of the tipping points for popularizing this capability.

➤ *MySpace and Facebook for work:* The phenomenon of personal publishing that the younger generation, including your teenagers and college students, will dramatically change people's expectations of how content and expertise are shared among colleagues. I predict the rise of totally new social networking systems and places where your workers can selectively and simply create their own views and capture their experiences. Imagine each employee with a rich profile that can be viewed by either the entire organization or a subnetwork of friends or colleagues. Imagine providing the workforce with a daily question rather than an answer and watching the responses rapidly shaping on a global basis, in real time. If you don't create a rich social networking space for your employees, they will create a covert one on their own!

➤ *Lifelong work and competency portfolios:* Although learning professionals have accepted the prediction that careers will span many jobs, there really isn't an easy method to make work experience or competencies portable. Imagine if a worker could earn targeted and micro merit badges that mapped to commonly accepted sets of key competencies that were part of a standardized competency dictionary. These would then be supported and contextualized by a career portfolio that would contain sanitized examples of work projects to provide backup and validation. These portfolios would be viewable within the company to better expose talent and capacities and could be selectively exposed externally as the workers sought their next jobs or positions.

➤ *More difficult and authentic assessment:* Too much e-learning assessment is designed for easy passing grades. Success rates are tracked on first usage at levels as high as 95 percent. Learners want to be challenged, and organizations deserve more difficult and authentic assessment. With the growth of gaming and simulation for learning, workers can be given the ability to fail forward, sometimes failing an assessment four or five times before they pass. When you are learning something new and difficult, failure is a natural and helpful part of the knowledge and skill acquisition process. Don't be afraid of ramping up the assessment intensity. It will engage learners better and yield far greater business impact.

Research and Development

There's a desperate need for a significant commitment to learning-focused research and development. I'd love to see a study showing the actual impact of long PowerPoint presentations. Instructors keep putting learners to sleep with slide hypnosis, but there is no research to inform this dysfunctional workplace habit. You need trusted, vendor-neutral studies on a range of learning topics, including the following:

➤ effectiveness of various e-learning models
➤ ideal duration of classes and online experiences
➤ role of multitasking on concentration, learning, and retention
➤ generational differences in learning
➤ effect of note-taking in classrooms and e-learning
➤ varied effectiveness of feedback and coaching strategies
➤ result of gaming on learning and retention
➤ impact of video and audio on learning and retention.

Such studies would help utilize e-learning technology for maximum efficiency. It is important to use studies that are available to you now and, based on your own project implementations, generate results that can be used within your organization for future learning projects.

Overcoming the Lies With Truth

Moving beyond the lies about e-learning requires you to demand greater truth telling from all parties. Learning professionals need to substitute measured evaluation for anecdotal stories. Move up Kirkpatrick's (1998) four-level evaluation model to look at true transfer to the workplace and business impacts. The instructional design models need to continuously evolve with changes in media, content creation, and the expectations of learners. And, you have to demand and listen to the truth from your learners. Figure out what actually helps your learners achieve and perform better in the workplace and what hinders the application of what they learn. Ultimately, the lie that must be overcome is a naïve belief that learning programs always work. When they do, it is a beautiful and powerful thing. When they don't, it is the job of learning professionals to figure out why and do something about it, even if it means admitting that they were taken in by all of the lies.

The Lie	The Truth
E-learning is new.	E-learning has been around for a very long time. Its beginnings can be traced to the advent of commercial radio in the 1920s and early experiments in using it to deliver classroom lessons to the children of rural farmers.
E-learning works!	There is an acute lack of reliable research and a large dose of fuzzy thinking about the actual effectiveness of specific e-learning programs. Workplace-based research on e-learning effectiveness must be funded so we can find out if e-learning works.
E-learning is just an online class.	Too much e-learning is a poor imitation of great instructor-led classes. Clinging to the classroom metaphor is limiting the benefits that could be obtained by exploiting the power and flexibility of e-learning.
E-learning pricing is sensible.	Pricing of e-learning content and learning systems is extremely confusing. Pricing for learning products and services needs a tune-up.
E-learning has a future.	E-learning is probably here to stay, but it will evolve according to trends in learning, technology, and society at large. Watch for the fading "e" and increasing media richness in e-learning experiences.

Reference

Kirkpatrick, D. (1998). *Evaluating Training Programs: The Four Levels* (2nd edition). San Francisco: Berrett-Koehler.

Lies About Learning Technology Tools

J.P. Lacombe

The irony of the current learning technology marketplace is that vendors still believe if they build it, you will come. How do I know this? Not long ago, I was a vendor consultant who was drinking and, admittedly, intoxicated by e-learning Kool-Aid. I couldn't get enough of the stuff! I read the pundit press; I read all the vendor marketing slicks I could get my hands on; I could speak e-learning jargon with the best of them. I loved it! I wrote about it, built it, and sold it. I was a card-carrying member of the vendor e-learning elite.

The learning technologies marketplace was (and still is) awash with the rhetoric of people like me; e-learning zealots who have been brainwashed to believe that authoring tools and learning management systems (LMSs) have revolutionized learning technologies. The fact is, corporate and academic professionals have studied, designed, built, and applied learning technology tools, including e-learning tools, for quite some time and were very successful before the e-learning Kool-Aid drinkers came along.

Now, I am in the process of atoning for my e-learning transgressions. I've hopped on the wagon and joined e-Learning Zealots Anonymous (eLZA). I bring these lies about learning technology tools and what to do about them as an offering to you on behalf of all the vendors who care to join me. On to the lies!

Lie #1: Customers Will Benefit From the Merger Through a Robust Product Offering.

While you watch from your customer seat in the coliseum of trade rags, investor news, and pundit publications, you see one vendor get tired of outpacing (or getting outpaced) by the others. So what do they do? They eat each other! They merge and acquire with the voracity of Roman lions. Merger of equals? Ha!

Whenever you see the word "robust" used in conjunction with a product or a service, beware. Truth be told, when a merger or acquisition happens, vendors don't want to share with you that they are not even close to working out the details of product integration. Interestingly, they may not have even discussed the details of a plan to merge the products by the time the press release announcing the deal comes out. It happens. It's the "build it and they will come" mentality; vendors are banking on the fact that you will want the new product, whatever it may be. It is a merged creation; it has to be good, right? Two ice cream scoops are better than one. Two minds working together are better than one. Two people screwing in a light bulb are better than one. The catalyst behind mergers and acquisitions is not thoughts of enhancing the product. Rather, the thinking is about market share increases and cost reductions. The bigger the market share, the higher the revenue, the better the possibility of profitability. Lower costs mean less money taken from revenues before it makes it to the bottom line. Investors love low costs and high profitability. I am a capitalist, too, but I'll square with you: Most mergers are in the best interests of the investors, not the customers.

Once a merger or acquisition happens, the first thing that comes to the vendor's mind is not "how are we going to merge these products"; it is reducing costs. Think of a merger or acquisition as a giant game of corporate "Survivor." After this game of outwit, outplay, and outlast shakes out, the vendor will then get down to the business of merging and integrating the products. This includes everything from marketing to software. More often than not, it is not the better product that wins out (that's what customers want); it is the product with the fewest flaws (reduced service costs) and better market opportunity (increased market share and revenues) that will survive.

The truth is that the company isn't truly attempting to benefit you, the customer, with the merger or acquisition. Eventually, when the business part of the business deal is done, software developers get to actually build something. That something usually is a new version of the product, which often is built from the ground up, using the best features and functionality of the previous product(s) as a baseline for development. This could take months or, in some cases, years to execute. Then, before the new product is even finished, the merger/acquisition cycle begins again. What happens to the customer base while all this is going on? You got it; you are offered a lot of e-learning Kool-Aid.

Here are some things to consider when you hear about a merger or acquisition that involves one of your key learning technology products:

➤ Has the vendor's salesperson stopped calling you since the merger or acquisition? If the salesperson has been calling you with less frequency after a merger or acquisition than before, it is likely he or she is unsure about what to say to you. This is a bad sign. If you want to (or need to) continue doing business with this vendor, call your salesperson immediately to establish a dialog about the change. If the conversation doesn't address your concerns, talk to someone more senior. If you still aren't satisfied, you may want to go to Plan B. No Plan B? A modicum of panic would be appropriate at this time.

➤ Does your salesperson express genuine confidence that this merger or acquisition is a good thing? A good salesperson, assuming you have a good relationship with him or her, won't pull any punches with you. He or she will tell you if the change is good for the company (and for you), because it will directly affect his or her livelihood if it is a bad deal. Don't be afraid to press on this issue. Be blunt. Ask "What does this mean for you (your earning potential) this year?" You will hear the doubt coming directly from the salesperson's wallet if there is a problem.

➤ Do you receive unsolicited, personal communication from senior company members? Three words for you: BIG RED FLAG. Senior management usually calls you because they are worried about negative perceptions surrounding the deal. This call comes under the guise of their concern for you as a customer. However, there is a silver lining in this conversation. If you are important enough ($$$) to warrant a call from senior management, you have leverage to influence them in your favor. This could come in the form of a discount, training, and so forth. Be creative. Ask what incentives you will be given to give your assurance that you will remain a customer. Keep pressing. Obviously, keep your own best interests in mind. After all, you have your own customers to serve.

In summary, mergers and acquisitions of tool vendors may or may not benefit you. The best way to handle these situations is to advocate on your own behalf. Remember, the best defense is a good offense. If you go on the offensive with your vendor, especially if you are considered a key customer, many of your concerns will be addressed. Rarely will a merger or acquisition be painless, but by actively partnering with your vendor, you should be able to make informed decisions about how it will affect your organization and what approach to take as a result.

Lie #2: The New Software Version of This Will Work With the Old Version.

This lie has been passed on by authoring tool vendors for 10 years, including the large operating system company whose name shall not be spoken. Typically, you discover this lie when you attempt to open a file that was created in a previous version of the software when using the new software. Sometimes the file won't open at all, and if it does, formatting or other information may be lost or inexplicably changed. You've heard of WYSIWYG (what you see is what you get)? Well, I call this frustrating experience WYSIWONT, because you won't be able to visualize the end result.

There has been much vendor carnage in the learning technology tool business. Remember AimTech's IconAuthor? AimTech was bought by Asymetrix, the makers of ToolBook, and IconAuthor was then summarily brought to an end in the interests of removing a competitor's product. Macromedia was purchased by Adobe; Docent and Click2learn have merged to become SumTotal systems; Saba bought

Centra and THINQ, and the list goes on and on. These examples are just the tip of e-learning tools consolidation. Many, many more companies, products, and people will be merged together to create new versions of products. It is difficult at best for companies to keep pedigreed product bloodlines. Darwin could have studied software development and could have come to the same conclusions as he did with evolution. Software companies should come clean with their customers: It is simply cost prohibitive to ensure future generations of software will work seamlessly with previous generations of software.

Salespeople will always push you to the next version of their company's product. But, the old adage "If it ain't broke, don't fix it" still applies here. If you are happy with the version of the software you are using, keep using it. It sounds simple, but there may be exceptions to this rule you need to be aware of. As I outlined previously, the software environment outside of your world will change and may force you to adapt to the change.

A popular example of this phenomenon is the issue of information security. Without applying security patches or even making upgrades to key software programs, especially web-based programs, you could be putting your organization at risk. Once again, become a product expert to the best of your abilities. Stay on top of the current issues and trends with the tools you are using or plan to use. Don't become enamored with a new feature that seems like a must-have, but then turns your existing files into WYSIWONT nightmares.

Lie #3: Our Products Conform to All Major E-Learning Standards.

Buyer: So this content will work on my platform?
Vendor: Of course. We are compliant with all relevant e-learning standards. Everything will be fine.

It is simply cost prohibitive to ensure future generations of software will work seamlessly with previous generations of software.

If you have been involved in purchasing an e-learning solution (or tool), you have probably been party to a conversation much like the preceding one. Unfortunately, much money has been spent learning the hard lesson that not all content works with all LMSs (or browsers for that matter) even if the content is e-learning standards compliant.

The now-familiar problem was that the different content formats didn't easily connect within the available infrastructure systems. Lack of integration and interoperability across the systems became a frustrating situation for users, requiring unexpected time and energy in the launch of an e-learning project. Many people got burned. The technology certainly didn't work as suppliers promised it would. There was much over-promising and even more under-delivering in the minds of many early purchasers. Service teams had to come to the rescue to knit components together, adding more time and expense.

The creation of development of standards is part of the maturation and legitimization of any industry. Standardization helps promote wide adoption by making the details of how things work together transparent to the user. Think of plug-and-play compatibility for computers and peripherals. Some believe standards will be the single most critical element in the success and adoption of e-learning in the future. Although I am all for the standards movement, it is premature to guarantee universal compatibility of learning content.

It's helpful to think of a standard as snapshots in time to help orient the marketplace so customers can compare apples to apples. Concern yourself with this question, "Which standards and which versions of those standards are you going to support and for what period of time?" The answer to this question is crucial. You have some homework to do to interpret and evaluate the answer to that question. Learn about standards and what your company's requirements are for meeting them. Think of your information reporting needs over time to ensure the product you buy is going to have some staying power. Research and anticipate the software environmental changes in your

Not all content works with all LMSs (or browsers for that matter) even if the content is e-learning standards compliant.

business. Ask your information technology (IT) department what its network and desktop configuration plans are going to be for the next several years. Be particularly wary if you have a distributed environment on which courses and an LMS will be separated by a firewall because most standards do not address firewall issues. The bottom line: Get on the same page as your IT organization. Most IT organizations know very little about e-learning standards. Good vendors can help you educate internal stakeholders if it enables the vendors to sell their products. Ask the following questions when beginning a dialog with your vendor's salesperson:

➤ What is the latest industry standard your product conforms to? (It helps to know a bit about industry standards before you ask.)

➤ Is this the latest standard on the market for this content or tool? (Again, you should know the answer before you ask.) If the product does not conform to the latest standard, ask why.

➤ Does anyone in your organization sit on the standards boards you support?

➤ How often do you update your content or tools based on standards changes in both the learning and software industries? (Pay special attention to web browser requirements, software plug-in requirements, and computer hardware requirements.)

➤ Do your new products have a history of working retroactively with prior standards?

➤ With which LMSs are you compatible? Can you show me the certifications? Are you a certified partner of any LMS vendors?

This list of questions is not exhaustive. More often than not, when asking these questions, you will exceed the breadth of the salesperson's product knowledge. Consequently, you need to talk to a product expert to get your answers. Ask to speak with one, and make sure you engage your IT organization in this conversation. If you have not exhausted the salesperson's knowledge, do some research; become a product expert yourself. At least learn enough to know when something doesn't sound right. Research can give you the ammunition you need to ask for guarantees, based on the needs and requirements of your software and hardware environment. Assuming there is a match between the vendor's requirements and yours, a performance guarantee should not be a problem.

Lie #4: There's No Need to Involve Your IT Department.

One way to slow down significantly, or worse, doom your investment in learning technology, is to exclude your company's IT organization from the procurement process. The best advice is to be a partner with IT staff and enlist their support early and often. For vendors, bringing your IT partner to the table is a double-edged sword. On the one hand, vendors want IT involved to speak to the people who helped design the network environment on which their software will run. On the other hand, vendors know how taxed IT departments can be and how conservative they are about allowing applications into their network environment. This is especially true of e-learning content that contains high-bandwidth audio and video or an LMS, which requires implementation behind your company's firewall.

Today's business applications require a solid IT network infrastructure and high bandwidth to carry information. Most progressive companies have already made significant investments in their network resources or are on the path to doing so. The typical issue IT has with e-learning tools is that they utilize network resources in a way that was not anticipated when creating the technology infrastructure. Most likely, your company's network was designed with only mission-critical applications and data in mind and was not designed to allow the movement of data associated with learning. E-learning programs that utilize audio and video need significant bandwidth; behind-the-firewall LMS solutions require significant resources for implementation and maintenance.

One way to slow down significantly, or worse, doom your investment in learning technology, is to exclude your company's IT organization from the procurement process.

Financial services, retail, and other industries that have traditionally relied upon existing infrastructure, such as phone lines, DSL, cable, or satellite to transmit information and face network traffic issues every day. Because these industries rely on an extensive service network, they have been challenged to move all their data from diverse locations around the country to central processing centers. It is not unheard of, even today, for these remote locations to rely on traditional telephone networks to move mission-critical information. In these cases, IT organizations keep a tight rein on the amount of data that is not mission-critical zipping across its networks. Downloading audio for an e-learning program in the middle of the workday certainly is not mission-critical to a remote bank branch or retail store connected to network via a telephone line. Processing transactions, however, is absolutely mission-critical.

This is one of the many reasons why a vendor might become uncomfortable about bringing IT to the table, especially if the vendor believes IT could inhibit a quick sale. It is also the reason why you can get locked out of your company's network if you bring it to a standstill because a couple hundred employees are trying to complete an e-learning program during business hours. The best advice I can give is to make a friend in IT well before you make plans to implement any type of learning technology solution, including hosted solutions.

Vendors will assure you that their application is bulletproof and does not take up much bandwidth. Take the time to learn as much as you can about your company's network infrastructure and demonstrate to your IT staff that you are working with them, not against them. Doing your homework and asking for help from IT will save you time and potential embarrassment when you go for that big e-learning or LMS solution you have been exploring.

Lie #5: Our Programs Will Work on All Current Browser Configurations.

This is classic e-learning sales speak. What this really means is, "Our programs will work on *most* browser configurations *that we have tested.*" You won't hear the words "we have tested" until you talk to the vendor's consultants and only then if you ask the right questions. Usually, by this point, you have been hooked and have invested too much time to call them on the lie and start over again with a new vendor. Want a good laugh? In a meeting attended by both your salesperson and a vendor consultant, watch the consultant's double-take after a salesperson tells this lie. The consultant will turn red, keep his or her mouth shut, and then blast the salesperson in the rental car (if they make it that far) for lying. This happens all the time.

The truth is that the vendor hasn't tested the program with *your* browser configuration. Make no mistake about it: Some issue will crop up when you are testing new learning tools on your network and on your machines. Configuration possibilities are nearly endless. This is why IT departments are so adamant about controlling the configuration of your computer. They know that if you introduce a new program onto the desktop or network environment that the environment can, and probably will, change. The vendor has tested its programs on a set of environments in its lab in an effort to catch as many possible configuration scenarios with a finite scope, budget, and timeframe. It is not feasible, from a business perspective, to test the entire universe of all environments to ensure compatibility with all configurations.

It is critical to engage your IT organization as early in the process as possible so it can pass on specifics to the vendor about your network environment, browser configurations, PC brands, servers, and so forth. It all matters. If your IT department has done its job well and the vendor has done its job well, the program you are buying should work with a minimal number of problems. If there are configuration compatibility issues, you can count on experiencing problems with implementation.

The best way to handle this lie is to make an apples-to-apples comparison of your environment and the vendor's technical requirements. How do your network configurations match to your vendor's hardware and software specifications? Press the salesperson to provide you with these requirements in detail and in writing. Do not settle for generic information such as MS Explorer 7.x. If the salesperson is evasive, ask to speak with an implementation consultant. Although the consultant is also motivated to make a sale, he or she also has to live with consequences of this lie. Therefore, the consultant is more likely to give you the information you need.

Do not become enamored with any one solution. You have to be willing to let go of a solution if it's incompatible with your network. Don't be duped by the corollary to this lie, that everything can be worked out during implementation. In most cases, that's just wishful thinking.

In the end, testing is the only surefire way to determine if your desired solution is going to work. Make testing a requirement of the procurement process and make any sale contingent on successfully passing the test. Reputable vendors will do this. They may not be happy about it, but they will recognize its ultimate value.

Overcoming the Lies With Truth

In fairness to all those vendor salespeople and consultants out there, most of them have not gone into selling learning technology to become rich, although I know many who have. They may believe their own lies, have been drinking the Kool-Aid, or are just trying to make a living. Just like any other technology, it's the infancy of the technology that creates the opportunity to lie. It is incumbent upon you, the consumer, to figure out what's the truth, what's a lie, and what lives somewhere in the middle.

The Lie	The Truth
Customers will benefit from the merger through a robust product offering.	The truth is that the company isn't truly attempting to benefit you, the customer, with the merger or acquisition. The best way to handle these situations is to advocate on your own behalf. By actively partnering with your vendor, you should be able to make informed decisions about how the merger/acquisition will affect your organization.
The new software version will work with the old version.	It is simply cost prohibitive to ensure future generations of software will work seamlessly with previous generations of software. So upgrade carefully and only after testing backwards compatiblity yourself.
Our products conform to all major e-learning standards.	Not all content works with all LMSs (or browsers for that matter) even if the content is e-learning standards compliant. You need to ask vendors the question, "Which standards and which versions of those standards are you going to support and for what period of time?"
There's no need to involve your IT department.	Doing your homework and asking for help from IT will save you time and potential embarrassment when you go for that big e-learning or LMS solution you have been exploring.
Our programs will work on all current browser configurations.	The truth is that the vendor hasn't tested the program with *your* browser configuration. Make no mistake about it: Some issues will crop up when you are testing new learning tools in your network and on your machines.

➤ 10

Lies About Learning to Lead

Kerry Johnson

Early in my career in the consulting and training business, my father would regularly ask me what I did for a living. Proudly, I would explain that I was in the business of helping leaders lead better. He would then respond, "That sounds nice but what exactly does it mean? Don't they already know how to lead? How did they get picked in the first place?" Undaunted and armed with the confidence of youth, I offered what I thought were compelling answers, most often based on some current project I was working on or some tidy leadership theory I fancied at the time. Once, for example, as I was about to launch a new collaboration course for frontline leaders, I told him that I had designed a program to help leaders work better with each other. "Oh!" he said, "Didn't they get picked to be leaders as far back as kindergarten just because they could play nicely with other kids? How can they learn to lead?"

Lie #1: The Big Lie: Leadership Can't Be Learned or Taught.

Underneath my father's questions lay the bigger question about learning to lead: Wasn't leadership something a person is born with and not something one can learn? After all, isn't it a complex and mysterious activity? Over the years, I've come to believe that many, many people agree with my father and support the idea that leaders are born, not made, and, consequently, leadership can't be learned. In my mind, this is the big lie about leadership learning. Even people who think leadership can be learned often believe that it can be learned only through experience. Coaching doesn't work. Leadership programs don't work. Only experience can be the teacher, and context, the coach.

If learning to lead is something that most people believe is difficult, if not impossible, why do so many learning professionals persist in trying to develop leaders and teach leadership? If leadership development is in the realm of possibility, how would you know that you've successfully taught someone to be a leader? What proof would there be? What measures? What methods might work? What could learning professionals do more (or less) to help others build their leadership capabilities? How does all this add up in the face of the big lie?

The fact is that leadership can be both learned and taught—a point I plan to drive home by the end of this chapter.

The Heroic Leader

It's almost a cliché among leadership gurus to say that the heroic model of leadership is disappearing because, even as we search for new ways to describe leadership, most people still seem to think of their leaders as heroes. Leaders are sought out as sources for protection, guidance, inspiration, and assurance. It is an archetypal pattern that goes back to the beginning of human history, drawing on metaphors such as the shepherd protecting the flock or the conqueror vanquishing the enemy at the border. People look to leaders for protection from real or imagined dangers. A rich literary culture of poetry, story, and song has evolved over centuries honoring leaders and heroes, often lifting them and their accomplishments beyond reality. In the process, the hero has not only been mythologized, but people have mythologized what it means to be a leader. They're expected to be heroes. As Sharon Daloz Parks (2005) writes, "Myth cannot be dismissed as mere fiction. Myths are epic, powerful stories that arise from, pervade, and shape the cultures we breathe." The myth becomes our reality.

I remember many years ago playing the part of Androcles in a community theater production of a children's play, *Androcles and the Lion*. After the show one day, I met a young child on the street afterward who wanted to know if I could help fix his brother's broken arm, "just like I'd helped the lion." Hero worship starts early and it continues into adulthood; it's not dependent upon reality.

The Power of Personality

Much of the hero myth lies in the fact that many of our leaders have strong and commanding personalities. Their presence is sensed to be bigger than life. Their language is captivating coupled with their power of expression and cemented by their use of symbols and metaphor. They appear to project power. This presence is recognized as a core trait of the leader.

Strong personality shows itself in many ways. Gandhi, Martin Luther King, and Mother Teresa, for example, were generally quiet people who led as much by example as by word. Gandhi said, "You must be the change you wish to see in the world." They were great with words, but they seemed to feel that words alone were insufficient to move people to new ways of behaving. By their example, they were heroic because they put their causes ahead of their own personal comforts, even to the point of sacrificing their own lives to the causes they believed in. Singleness of purpose was one of their greatest strengths.

Strong personality can also be displayed in bulldog tenacity (Sir Winston Churchill), brilliant intellect (Albert Einstein), or clarity of vision (President Abraham Lincoln). In each case, these leaders were able to influence people through a set of personal characteristics and strengths that seem beyond most of us. Their personality and character alone speak of heroism, even when their deeds falter. How can you learn that? How can you learn to be a hero?

Charisma and Context

In the era of television, personal dynamism and charisma seem more important than ever. Charisma plays right into the lie of the born leader because so much of the leader's power is conveyed through his or her physical characteristics as well as from an ability to use the media effectively. Even before television, the public fell victim to what Malcolm Gladwell (2005) refers to as the "Warren Harding Error." President Warren G. Harding was a tall, powerful, handsome man who looked every inch a president. People believed he was presidential, so they nominated and elected him. According to Gladwell, most historians agree that Harding was a terrible president, although he sure looked the part of a great leader. Television tends to diminish a leader who does not appear to look presidential or senatorial or like a chief executive officer (CEO). Looks count, and looks are something you're born with.

A great example of the use of charisma and context is the Cold War image of President Reagan standing before the Brandenburg Gate in Berlin saying "Mr. Gorbachev, tear down this wall!" The powerful combination of his simple words spoken in the setting of the wall dividing East and West Germany made him look and sound heroic. Reagan was the great communicator not only because he knew how to use clear and simple language, but also because he was able to combine his movie-star good looks with visual symbols that amplified his words. How can that be learned or taught?

Authority and Leadership

Finally, a big piece of the hero myth comes from the concept of authority. It's part of the self-fulfilling prophecy that people in power are in power because they are born leaders. Once they are in a position of authority (president, CEO, boss, chair, or captain), people respond to them simply because of their role. They become heroes because of their position and the hope instilled in them to provide safety and assurance.

But, leadership is much more than position and power. "Leadership is the art of mobilizing others to want to struggle for shared aspirations" (Kouzes & Posner, 1995, p. 30). People in authority are expected to provide direction and norms that help a group work toward its goals. That is vital but not sufficient in helping mobilize others to struggle for shared aspirations. Leadership is more about helping people move beyond familiar patterns to tackle their toughest problems. It is not enough to solve merely technical problems, but the leader's work is to deal with the most complex issues facing him or her and the organization. This often involves questioning values, taking great personal risk, and letting go of long-standing beliefs, and often control, to find a new way of achieving an acceptable outcome (Heifetz, 1994).

Heifetz refers to these kinds of complex problems as adaptive challenges. When the focus shifts from authority and technical problems to leadership and adaptive challenges, the personal traits of the leader—personality, charisma, and so forth—become less important. What becomes more important is the leader's ability to be present, to see the complexity of the situation, and to intervene appropriately.

The hero myth supports the lie that leaders are born not made because it credits the leader's success with exceptional, even supernatural power, strength, or intelligence. Physical characteristics, charisma, and role authority all contribute to reinforcing the hero myth. What the hero myth overlooks is the importance of the critical and learnable behaviors that leaders employ in using power, uncovering strength, or applying intelligence. It also shortchanges the importance of context in shaping the leader's behavior. Without a context, it is possible that a leader will never find his or her ultimate power or strength or intelligence.

Lie #2: The Leader Must Bring About Change Alone.

At dawn on April Fool's Day, 1993, Lou Gerstner stood outside a locked office building trying to figure out how to get in so he could begin his tenure as IBM's new CEO. He was invited to join a meeting of senior global sales executives. No one anticipated that he would be unable to enter the building. The meeting proved an excellent initiation into the entrenched bureaucracy, fiefdoms, and political infighting within IBM and a clear picture of the challenges awaiting Gerstner in his effort to restore the company to its glory days (Gerstner, 2002).

But, there were big changes in the computing industry in the late 1980s and early 1990s. Increased competition from other mainframe companies, coupled with a push toward workstations, PCs, and distributed computing, led to the impression that IBM was neither keeping up with competition nor with technology shifts. The impact on IBM was a falloff in mainframe sales, loss of credibility with chief information officers (CIOs), and a loss of confidence that IBM had the customers' best interests in mind in the sales organization. And, IBM stock dropped from a high of $43 in 1987 to $12 in 1993. No one was happy.

Without doubt, Gerstner faced what Heifetz (1994) would call an adaptive challenge. This was no mere technical problem. Changes in markets, competitors, technologies, and customer expectations were forcing IBM to confront its values, develop new strategies, and learn new ways of operating. Adaptive work is required when deeply held beliefs are challenged, when the values that once brought success become less relevant, and when legitimate yet competing perspectives emerge (Gerstner, 2002).

Adaptive change requires individuals throughout the organization to change, which is why adaptive leadership is integral to the entire process. The complexity of the challenge can only be addressed through collective imagination. People from across the organization need to be engaged in addressing the issues both from the perspective of their own expertise and from their ability to work together. Leaders must anticipate and be ready to work through resistance, which is a natural part of change. According to Heifetz and Linsky (2002, p. 11), "People don't resist change. They resist loss." The leader needs to let go of the problem and give the work back to the people. People at all levels of the organization need to solve the problem. The leader, then, is in a position of asking questions, not answering them. He or she must do the hard work of pushing people to think harder, question values, and seek alternatives that they might never have previously considered viable. The leader must encourage conflict rather than simply diffuse it.

For most leaders this form of participative, collaborative, and adaptive behavior is very difficult. It means that the leader must be both in the action and above it or, to use a Ron Heifetz phrase, both "on the dance floor and on the balcony." By that, he means that the leader must be able to simultaneously take part in the action and step back from it so that he or she can see the patterns of the action. It is the ultimate example of action and reflection.

The leader, then, is in a position of asking questions, not answering them. He or she must do the hard work of pushing people to think harder, question values, and seek alternatives that they might never have previously considered viable. The leader must encourage conflict rather than simply diffuse it.

Leading change also involves regulating the distress that people feel as they change to meet the challenges they face. People cannot learn new behaviors when they're overwhelmed, but an appropriate amount of stress can motivate change.

Clearly, higher-order thinking and adaptive leadership are complex and difficult to learn. It is also not hard to see why most people feel they are impossible to teach. That's especially true considering standard models for teaching and learning. Other than some form of natural selection, how do people get better at this? How did Lou Gerstner, Churchill, Gandhi, or any adaptive leaders know how to lead like this? They were smart, no doubt. They were committed. But, how were they able to apply their own natural gifts to evolve as leaders and thinkers?

Lie #3: Telling People Clearly What to Do Is the Key to Adaptive Change.

What is the core work of leaders and how does it relate to the idea of adaptive leadership? Lou Gerstner's adaptive leadership style is certainly appropriate at the CEO level, but his success resulted from his ability to develop adaptive leaders at all levels of the IBM organization. How does the core work of leaders vary from level to level? What are the specific skills and behaviors to look for in leaders throughout the company and how can you build a pipeline of leaders? I will address these and other questions below.

Leaders at all levels of an organization are required to do several core things (figure 10-1). The first of these is to establish direction and align their team in relation to the strategy of the firm. The second is to build the commitment and capability of their team to execute the plan. The third is to execute the plan and provide performance feedback for ongoing improvement. At the heart of the three core activities are the personal behaviors and traits that enable the leader to succeed. These include self-mastery, communication and interpersonal skills, and values and beliefs.

Direction and Alignment

Like a good rowing team, high-performing organizations need everyone to pull in the same direction and in unison. Pulling in the same direction

Figure 10-1. The work of leaders.

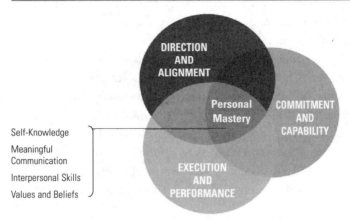

Self-Knowledge
Meaningful
Communication
Interpersonal Skills
Values and Beliefs

Source: 2006 IIR Holdings, Ltd. All rights reserved. The Forum Corporation of North America, Authorized Licensee.

requires a clear line of sight to the company strategy from every vantage point. The leader must know how to interpret that strategy at both the team and individual level. Because it is each leader's responsibility to ensure that everyone has a clear line of sight to the strategy, the strategy will be successful if and only if there are leaders at all levels of the organization that understand and accept the adaptive challenge.

Commitment and Capability

Leadership capability is generally considered in terms of competency models that describe the knowledge, skills, and abilities required to lead. Individuals are assessed against these models, gaps in their performance identified, and specific training recommended. Although the premise seems sound and the approach straightforward, it represents only part of the solution to either individual or organizational effectiveness. Individual knowledge, skills, or abilities by themselves do not lead to effectiveness. Commitment to the corporate vision and strategy is also important and that has driven more factors in the organizational culture and climate. This commitment–capability relationship is complex and interdependent. One without the other can cause both the individual and the organization to fail.

The typical competency model and gap analysis approach to leadership development doesn't deliver the impact on organizational effectiveness that senior leaders seek. The competency model approach is focused on improving specific knowledge, skills, and abilities that are more often based on technical problems for which the solutions are straightforward. If the real work of leaders involves adaptive challenges, then the individual development approach must be combined with an organizational leadership development cycle.

In short, leadership development requires a systems perspective. Just as a company spends time, attention, and money creating processes and systems to ensure product innovation and quality, it needs to create processes and systems to develop leadership talent. These include not only training for individuals, but also creating support systems throughout the organization that reinforce and complement training.

Execution and Performance

A good strategy is worthless without a focus on execution. Leaders at all levels of the organization need to create a clear line of sight to the strategy and consistently monitor progress. Leaders must address the constant evolution of strategic direction and the need to keep employees fully informed and strategically linked. Research by The Forum Corporation indicates that less than 5 percent of the typical workforce understands the organization's strategy. With no knowledge of how their work contributes to the success of the organization, employees are less engaged and committed and organizational performance deteriorates.

An adaptive leader involves employees in strategic discussions and establishes a clear line of sight from the employees' work—activities that are critical to the success of the organization and essential in today's rapidly changing environment. Helping employees maintain clarity and focus is an important way to ensure they are engaged in activities that make the most contribution to the success of the organization. Therefore, effective leaders take seriously their role in providing direction for employees' work and linking it to the larger organizational strategy.

The formal performance management processes of the organization are one way to achieve linkage; traditional, once-a-year performance planning, however, is no longer sufficient for helping employees make adjustments to help the organization's strategy adapt to market changes. In fast-changing, knowledge-reliant work environments, leaders must be constantly aligning and realigning their teams' and team members' work with their organizations' strategy. In environments where employees are dispersed and assignments too diverse to sustain close supervision, leaders must constantly build employee motivation by providing meaning for their valuable work. In addition, today's highly interdependent organizations require leaders to integrate the needs of other organizational entities, inside and outside the firm, into their own work plans and objectives.

Successful leaders recognize that creating clarity and focus is an ongoing task. As a result they work to build coaching and learning into everyday work. They know that, when people have a deep, intimate, and ongoing understanding of how they contribute to the business strategy, their creativity, knowledge, and commitment are unleashed in the service of the organization.

The Limits of Competency Models

Technical work is really about applying current know-how to solve problems, and the people in authority—leaders, in the traditional sense—can do that work. Adaptive work requires new ways of thinking and doing things, and people dealing with the problem are the only ones capable of doing that. In short, a leader doing adaptive work must have skills and capabilities beyond those found in traditional competency models or addressed through typical training and development. Heifetz and Linsky (2002) go so far as to say that "the single most common source of leadership failure we've been able to identify—in politics, community life, business, or the nonprofit sector—is that people, especially those in positions of authority, treat adaptive challenges like technical problems."

Adaptive work is clearly context specific. As a result, one of the more effective ways of helping someone learn how to lead change is through one-on-one coaching. A good coach is always sensitive to the context when assessing competencies. A set of competencies that works under one set of circumstances can often lead to trouble in another context. The coach often asks evocative questions that get the leader to speculate about or evaluate the situation and his or her own behaviors in new and different ways, or the questions provoke the leader to explore feelings of those involved in the situation. Most leaders with traditional graduate training are very strong analytically. They might even be strong strategically. What they often lack, however, is the competencies that allow them to see things from a fresh perspective or explore things from another's point of view. This is where a good executive coach is worth his or her fee.

So, given that leadership is complex and mysterious, demanding and difficult, how can it possibly be learned or taught? Accepting that the work of the leader at all levels of the organization is adaptive work, what would it take to learn to lead? How can it be done? Who can teach it? What would they do to teach it? What is the individual leader's role in learning to lead? Where does the organization fit? What would success look like for the leader or for the organization?

Lie #4: A Decision to Change Is All That Is Required to Make Change Happen.

Organization-wide change is a gradual, phase-by-phase process that must be carefully balanced and monitored along the way. The first challenge in learning to lead is to understand that learning is about personal change, and change is about letting go. When he realized that he was not facing a technical problem, but an adaptive challenge, Lou Gerstner knew that he would personally need to change. Even more than that, he knew every one of his leaders, at every level of the organization, would need to change. His experience as a management consultant at McKinsey was not going to help. Even his tenure as CEO at American Express couldn't prepare him for this challenge. He needed to think differently, and he needed to get each leader in IBM to think differently. It was not about his expertise or theirs. It was about engaging the people—the entire leadership of IBM, from top to bottom—with the adaptive challenge they faced and working with them to learn new ways of thinking and behaving (figure 10-2).

Figure 10-2. Learning to be.

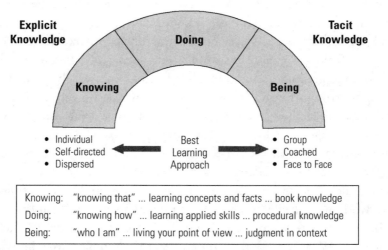

Knowing:	"knowing that" ... learning concepts and facts ... book knowledge		
Doing:	"knowing how" ... learning applied skills ... procedural knowledge		
Being:	"who I am" ... living your point of view ... judgment in context		

Leading adaptive work requires people to be different. This is not only about knowing new things and ways of thinking. It is also about developing and using new behaviors. Most important, it is about developing a new mindset, a new way of seeing the world.

Getting on the edge requires leaving your comfort zone. Most leadership training plays with this idea instead of practicing it relentlessly. It is about stretch. It's about trying new things, not once or twice, but over and over again until those new things become second nature. It's not just about the practitioner; it's also about the group and the context within which the practice is done.

Leadership boils down to changing other peoples' behavior, in addition to your own. By approaching learning as a change process, leaders not only gain a much better sense of the inherent difficulties in changing their own behavior, but also the difficulties in changing others' behavior. Change is not easy. In life or death situations, ones in which a doctor has definitively determined that unless you changed some behavior you would die, the scientifically studied odds are nine to one (!) against your doing so (Parks, 2005). Even in this dire scenario, people must find some comfort in preserving the status quo.

A senior leader at a major Canadian bank once described to me his frustration with most leadership training. He said that as a middle-aged man he'd learned to ski and to play golf so that he could spend more time with his grown kids. They liked to do those things and he wanted to be with them, so he took up both sports. He said that learning to play those sports changed his life. He never walked past a magazine rack without looking at golf or skiing magazines, and he started to meet new people who enjoyed skiing and golfing, too. He had different conversations with colleagues and friends. In short, he became totally involved in each sport. He continually pushed himself in a way that he became a skier and a golfer. He didn't just learn about them. "Why is it," he asked me with some concern, "that learning to lead is not made to be as all-consuming and as mind altering? Why do we think we can do it in a three-day class? How can we hope to transform a person's thinking so that he or she can emerge a leader?"

For this leader, as for Gerstner, learning became a personal change process. As such, each added new knowledge to his repertoire, helping him change core behaviors and becoming what he wanted to become. How did they do it? They got on the edge. They put themselves in new and uncomfortable situations, tried new ways of thinking and acting, sought adaptive challenges, and observed themselves carefully to see how they and others responded to those new situations and challenges. In short, they became comfortable with their own discomfort.

Given the long odds against changing your behavior and becoming someone new, especially in challenging situations, how can you be expected to get on the edge to change yourself? You can't hope to change unless at least three things happen. First, you need to be put into a situation in which you are forced to try new behaviors and shift your mindset. You need to put yourself on the edge or to have someone else put you on the edge in spite of yourself. This requires a safety net of some sort, but it also requires acceptance of risk. You need to feel explicitly and precisely what you're letting go of, and what the new behavior or attitude is going to be like when done correctly. Heifetz and Linsky (2002) refer to this experience as a holding environment. It's like a life lab: a safe, controlled, and challenging environment within which to fail and learn from failure as well as to succeed and learn from success.

Second, you need strong feedback loops. To learn from either failure or success you must get the kind of constant and corrective information that allows you to tune your performance and learn the new ways properly. This can be a combination of personal reflections and coaching from others. No one learns only by staring in the mirror. People learn by being challenged and guided by others who are able to point out differences between their assumptions and their actual behaviors and inspire change challenge experiences and offer advice on new ways forward.

Third, the learning characteristics of the holding environment must extend to the workplace. To accomplish that, the climate of the organization needs to support practice of new approaches, reward risk taking, and encourage constructive criticism. When you put these three things together, they look like figure 10-3. Under normal circumstances, these are not typical characteristics in the corporate workplace. They need to be fostered in a purposeful way.

Figure 10-3. The integrated learning model.

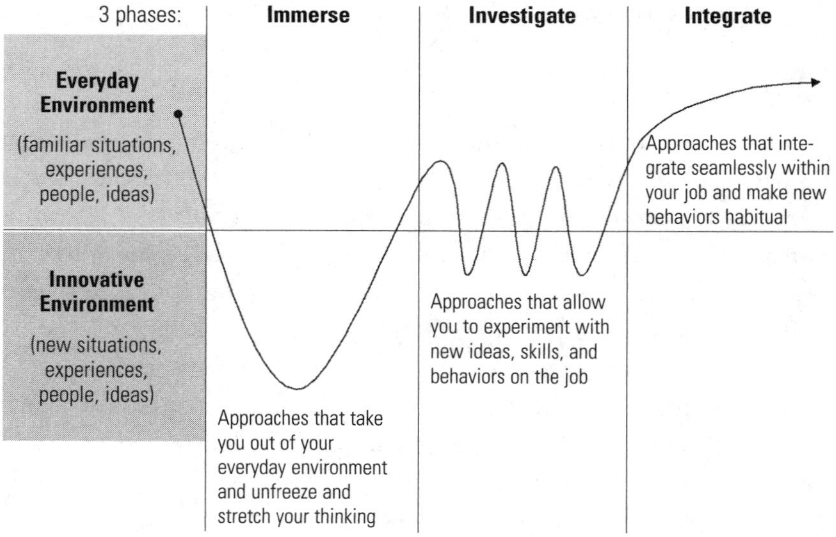

Source: 2006 IIR Holdings, Ltd. All rights reserved. The Forum Corporation of North America, Authorized Licensee.

Periods of immersion, investigation, and integration allow the leader to get on the edge and try out new ideas and behaviors in progressively more challenging and complex ways. Learning is never removed from the realities of work, yet the holding environment allows for safe experimentation that fosters risk taking and behavioral change. It pushes emerging leaders out of their comfort zone, challenging their beliefs. It forces them not only to see leadership differently, but also to experience themselves differently.

Leaders work intensely within the immersion phase so the power of the new ideas and skills can be appreciated and habituated. During the investigation, phase leaders use the new concepts and practices in real work situations while relying on regular coaching and feedback from peers, managers, and direct reports to fine-tune performance. They also perfect their own ability to reflect on performance and provide their own feedback. Finally, during the integration phase, leaders concentrate on making the new ideas and abilities part of their normal repertoire.

Creating a Holding Environment

Because the process of engaging people at the edge of learning is designed to challenge long-held beliefs and assumptions, it can be uncomfortable. In many ways, the holding environment resembles a therapist's office. It is a place to confront your own realities during this deep and challenging work. In the immersion phase, people react in many ways. Sometimes they confront the instructor and the group. Other times they withdraw. The instructor's role is to regulate the heat (Heifetz & Linsky, 2002). He or she must understand the tolerance of the group for stretch and stress and adjust accordingly. Most important, the instructor must make sure there is heat. There is a natural tendency to avoid the work. How often have you heard participants in a leadership program balk at doing role plays or exercises? How often have you heard them say, "I know this already, let's get on with it!" How often have they suggested that practice is a waste of time?

A successful holding environment allows the learner to establish a sense of inclusion to recognize the relevance of issues confronted and develop confidence in his or her own ability to become a leader. Each of these is an important component of the holding environment. Without them it is simply not possible to productively challenge participants.

The instructor's task in establishing a holding environment is to create a living laboratory within which participants can try on new ideas and behaviors and react to others who are doing the same thing. The artistry for the instructor is to create activities that enable the group to act as living examples of the concepts he or she is trying to get across. This is beyond discovery learning in that whatever the discoveries they are likely to have been unknown to both participant and instructor before the session.

As an instructor in this kind of a learning lab setting, you are challenged to model the behaviors you seek. This is very different from having content to communicate, goals to accomplish, or an agenda to adhere to. Learning in a holding environment like this is hard work for everyone, especially since the final destination is as unclear to the instructor as it is to the participants. Without cue cards or scorecards, both instructor and student feel the heat.

The Dance Floor and the Balcony

Heifetz refers to this method of teaching adaptive leadership as the "case-in-point" (Deutschman, 2005). The class becomes its own laboratory. Actions and reactions of participants become the raw materials of learning. Reflections on those actions drive new learning. It is an approach that involves tremendous self-awareness, honesty, and planning, both on the part of the instructor and the participants. Activities are designed to put participants in situations where they become aware of specific concepts by actively participating in those concepts. The instructor orchestrates activities that invite people to try on new ways of performing, push their own limits, and evaluate their peers. It is a demanding role for an instructor and not one to be taken lightly. It is challenging for participants who are never let off the hook to be completely present and accountable.

Most leadership training does not approach this level of introspection, immersion, or stretch. Leaders are too polite and are too eager to avoid conflict. Consequently, too much accommodation is provided.

The technique Heifetz uses to help participants live their learning role successfully is to have them think about simultaneously being on the dance floor and on the balcony observing the dance. The dance floor and the balcony become metaphors about a lifelong study of leadership. It also makes the important case for both being in the flow and able to disassociate from the flow in order to observe.

A leader's biggest trap is not letting go of the work. They are so involved that they're not mindful of what is being done or their role in the doing. Bill Russell, the great Boston Celtics center, used to say that when the game was going perfectly he felt as though he was able to rise above it and watch it happen. He said he could anticipate where he needed to be and what he and his teammates would do next. It is a level of self-reflection that does not come naturally. It needs to be consciously considered and practiced.

Most traditional leadership training does not leave the time for this level of reflection. In my own work, I am constantly pushing myself to make room for reflection, and in my designs for leadership programs I force myself to leave space for reflection and silence. Today's culture is action oriented. No one likes slowing down, but the truth is you have to slow down to go fast.

During the investigation and integration phases of the learning model, the dance floor and the balcony are also important concepts. Often they are hard to remember, however. To get more from either the dance floor or the balcony, I try to have someone along for the ride. This person can observe and provide the kind of feedback that encourages experimentation, challenges assumptions, and keeps the heat on. One reason for the declining impact of traditional learning programs is the lack of the incentive to practice and absence of coaching opportunities that will make a difference for the long term.

Lie #5: Talk Is Cheap. It's Action That Demonstrates Leadership.

Yes, it is really important to try on new leader behaviors to be effective in applying them, but, as a colleague of mine is fond of saying, "The conversation is the work." Whatever's accomplished in the modern organization gets done through conversations with one another. When work was individual and craft-oriented, conversation was less important. Even in the industrial age with its leaders and follows, command and control, bosses and workers, union and management, conversation was less important than clear directions and orders. Even 20 years ago, lag time was tolerable. Following a misunderstanding, people could reconnect and set each other straight. There was recovery time.

At today's pace, the work is often in the moment and any clarification needs to occur immediately through skillful conversation or dialog. Knowledge needs to be communicated at the speed of the change, which in information-age organizations is likely to be immediate. Look at the direction software is taking. Microsoft focuses totally on enabling the power of people by making it easier and easier to work together through their software. The whole purpose of their soon-to-be-released operating system is to allow the kind of virtual conversation that speeds the creation and impact of work output.

As a result, a core capability of leaders is the ability to communicate and converse. I can't remember a market needs analysis done at The Forum in the last 20 years that didn't cite communication as anything other than one of the top two or three learning needs of an organization. Push people to find out what they mean by communication. They'll say it's about the conversation, and more than anything, it's about conversations that change people. They report that most conversations in their organization are about exchanging information, while their most critical needs involve getting things done by changing the way people are approaching the effort.

One of the most challenging leadership skills involves deep communication at the level of dialog. Change requires the kind of deep conversation that affects people's attitudes, beliefs, and eventually their actions. Leaders must explore their understanding of themselves, their employees, and their organization through dialog. Turn up the heat by pressing them to deal with the real issues they face day in and day out and discuss them openly and honestly. These are typically difficult conversations. In a case-in-point approach to learning, the challenge for the instructor is to keep the people in the room on task, working the issues, pushing for clarity, and revealing their own biases.

The interesting thing about this emphasis on conversation and dialog is that most people have difficulty doing it effectively. People are hardwired to tell and sell, not to facilitate a real conversation or dialog. There are specific skills required to conduct an effective conversation. Most leaders know them. They can often even tell you what they are, but they still can't do them.

Dialog and conversation are at the core of The Forum's leadership approach. Learning firms that understand the way people really work together are passionate about making the conversation central to the work and learning. When Heifetz talks about creating a holding environment, the most significant component of that environment is that it enables dialog and conversation. In fact, a goal of the holding environment is to provide a place where you can orchestrate conflict and use the tools of dialog to work through that conflict in constructive ways. One way to regulate the heat is to add varying amounts of conflict and allow participants to work through the conflict in ways that provide practice in using the skills necessary in adaptive work.

Unfortunately, most leadership training fails to address the importance of creating a holding environment or orchestrating conflict or providing challenges that drive dialog. It fails to mirror the realities of adaptive work, rendering it ineffective.

Lie #6: Leaders Must Only Celebrate Successes to Encourage Organizational Learning.

It's important to learn from failures as well as successes. In fact, failure is often the best teacher. When you are open to that idea, it is astonishing how much you can learn. Learning professionals are very comfortable looking at best practices for guidance. They help. Plenty can be learned from best practices, but the most lasting learning often comes from failure.

The armed forces are great at learning from mistakes. In fact, they've made an art form of it. Their mantra seems be "we should never make the same mistake twice." They use many techniques to learn from their mistakes including after-action reports and embedded observers. When the infantry goes on maneuvers, officers are assigned to make careful observations of everything that takes place from tactics to conversations. Often these are people whose only task is to observe the action carefully. They debrief quickly and completely. No detail is left unexamined. They thrive on mistakes as lessons.

Why is this so hard in other organizations? Why don't we use after-action reports or embedded observers in business? Even in a training environment, this can be a threat. The main reason is that businesses and business leaders don't like to admit their mistakes. The higher you rise in an organization, the less likely you are to want to expose any personal weaknesses. There might be reprisals. Bonuses are on the line. Wall Street might react. Leaders might look bad.

If there is any place in business that people receive useful feedback that they can apply to improve performance, it is in annual reviews. However, most performance reviews are too little, too late. In fact, they seldom address issues with the kind of skilled diagnosis and prescription that can lead to improvement. Instead, either they offer passing positive reinforcement and a light touch on suggestions for improvement, or they come as a warning to shape up—or else. A fair amount of time is spent teaching managers how to conduct performance reviews, but as people rise through the organization it is assumed that they either already have that skill or they are just naturals. In many cases, neither is correct.

At The Forum Corporation, people discuss building learning into everyday work. People are taught to become excellent at both giving and receiving feedback, but teaching people to think like that requires a real transformation. In fact, learning itself is a transformation that takes place over time (Collins, 2002). Building learning into everyday work is not a mindset or skill set that can be instilled in leaders in a single class. It requires a fully integrated learning approach, which most organizations are either unwilling to invest the time in or are not convinced that much time is required. I can't remember how many times I've had a client who I generally respect tell me "we have a really smart bunch of people here so it shouldn't take them that long to learn to coach." It's a skill that even the smartest people require time to learn.

Overcoming the Lies With Truth

People like to think of their leaders as being honorable, trustworthy, and credible. They should be courageous and curious, and they should be able to inspire those emotions in those whom they lead. A quote attributed to Antoine de Saint-Exupéry, the French pilot and author, sums this up perfectly: "If you want to build a ship, don't drum up people to collect wood and don't assign them tasks and work, but rather teach them to long for the endless immensity of the sea."

According to Jim Collins (2001), successful leaders are all about personal humility and fierce resolve. All leaders aspire to those traits. It is obvious that they are difficult traits to learn, but, as I've tried to show, people can learn to develop those traits and learn to lead. We can teach people to lead. However, doing so requires a whole different approach to learning and teaching than we typically see in a corporate environment. To teach leadership you must lead. To learn leadership you must lead. You can't teach about leadership. You can't learn about leadership. You must lead to become a leader, both in the classroom and on the job.

Learning to lead this way is based on four critical design criteria and subsequent actions on the part of the instructor. Each learning environment must do the following:

➤ *Establish inclusion.* Learners must feel they're not only part of the class, but also responsible for the class. Inclusion in this case means that each individual takes ownership for the success or failure of the group's learning as well as his or her own learning.

➤ *Establish relevance.* Everything must point directly back to the job. Why is this important to me? How will I use these ideas, skills, and approaches? The gifted instructor will be able to create a container within which learning can take place in a personally relevant way. As for the learners, they will need to reveal enough of themselves to recognize the relevance of the experience.

➤ *Create involvement.* Participants must be on the dance floor and on the balcony. There is no way to learn to lead except by leading. The instructor must give the work of the class back to the class, just as he or she wants the leader to give the work of the organization back to the people being led.

➤ *Develop confidence.* Participants need to emerge from the learning experience knowing that they have tried to apply new skills and behaviors in realistic conditions and can actually apply them in the workplace. If they've failed at anything, they need to know what they learned from that failure. If they've succeeded, they need to celebrate that success in the way Collins would anticipate a level 5 leader to celebrate—humbly and with resolve to do better next time. Most of all, they need to feel comfortable with silence, secure in giving work back to the people, and confident that no matter how well they did there is always room to improve.

How do you know when you've succeeded in developing a leader? The ultimate test of success in leadership learning is that leaders learn to develop other leaders. Jack Welch's real success as a leader is often measured by the number of senior executives at other firms who learned from him at GE. Most of these ex-GE leaders, such as Larry Bossidy, for example, applied Welch's approaches. They made learning a critical strategic activity. They personally followed up to see that people were learning. And, perhaps most important, they used themselves as examples. Teaching others to lead became a cornerstone of their leadership style. By becoming students of leadership and consciously evaluating their own behaviors as leaders, Welch and Bossidy were able to develop leaders throughout their organizations. By combining an emphasis on training and development and by modeling the behaviors they sought throughout their organizations, they were able to create a climate of leadership. They address the complexity and mystery of leadership head on.

Willa Cather wrote in 1915 that "There are some things you learn best in calm, and some in storm" (p. 274). By creating a culture of leadership day by day across an organization, you can create the kind of calm and storm required for learning. Leadership can be learned. It can also be taught. It's not as easy as we'd like to think, but it can be done.

The Lie	The Truth
Leadership can't be learned or taught.	The fact is that leadership can be both learned and taught.
The leader must bring about change alone.	People from across the organization need to be engaged in addressing the issues both from the perspective of their own expertise and from their ability to work together.
Telling people clearly what to do is the key to adaptive change.	An adaptive leader involves employees in strategic discussions and establishes a clear line of sight from the employees' work—activities that are critical to the success of the organization and essential in today's rapidly changing environment. Adaptive leaders nurture development of other leaders at all levels within the organization.
A decision to change is all that is required to make change happen.	Organization-wide change is a gradual, phase-by-phase process that must be carefully balanced and monitored along the way. Periods of immersion, investigation, and integration allow the leader to get on the edge and try out new ideas and behaviors in progressively more challenging and complex ways.
Talk is cheap. It's action that demonstrates leadership.	"The conversation is the work." A core capability of leaders is the ability to communicate and converse. Whatever's accomplished in the modern organization gets done through conversations with one another.
Leaders should celebrate successes to encourage organizational learning.	Plenty can be learned from best practices, but the most lasting learning often comes from failure. Although businesses don't like to admit their mistakes, failure can be the best teacher.

References

Cather, W. (1915, republished in 2000). *The Song of the Lark. Oxford's World Classics.* New York: Oxford University Press, USA.

Collins, J. (2001). *Good to Great: Why Some Companies Make the Leap...and Others Don't.* New York: HarperCollins.

Deutschman, A. (2005, May). "Change or Die." *Fast Company,* 53–62.

Gerstner, L.V. (2002). *Who Says Elephants Can't Dance? Inside IBM's Historic Turnaround.* New York: HarperCollins.

Gladwell, M. (2005). *Blink: The Power of Thinking Without Thinking.* New York: Little, Brown and Company.

Heifetz, R.A. (1994). *Leadership Without Easy Answers.* Boston: Harvard University Press.

Heifetz, R.A., and M. Linsky. (2002). *Leadership on the Line: Staying Alive through the Dangers of Leading.* Boston: Harvard Business School Press.

Kouzes, J., and B. Posner. (1995). *The Leadership Challenge: How to Keep Getting Extraordinary Things Done in Organizations* (2nd edition). San Francisco: Jossey-Bass.

Parks, S.D. (2005). *Leadership Can Be Taught: A Bold Approach for a Complex World.* Boston: Harvard Business School Press.

Lies About Learning Organizations

Steven P. Ober

Lies and Liars

In every major management movement—management by objectives, participatory management, total quality, business process reengineering, and organizational learning—many lies have been told. To be fair, most of the lies are born of ignorance rather than malice. They are unintentional lies told by good people who want to believe that what they are saying is true. Sadly, a few of the lies are told intentionally by people who want to gain some advantage, say, by landing a large consulting contract. Unfortunately, most liars, whether their intentions are good or bad, convince themselves that their lies are true.

Often, after conversations about becoming a learning organization (LO), it is sometimes unclear what was said, who promised what, what was being sold, or what was being bought. If it's unclear what happened, it's impossible to know what results the activities produced. The

---

To be fair, most of the lies are born of ignorance rather than malice. They are unintentional lies told by good people who want to believe that what they are saying is true.

---

only thing anyone is sure about after a project like that is a great deal of money was spent and everyone is exhausted. Such is the world of organizational learning and change.

To be truthful (what a concept!), articles, methods, models, designs, and sales pitches notwithstanding, no one really knows how to do organizational learning or to pull off a successful, large-scale organizational change. As they say, "In the land of the blind, the one-eyed person is king." So, let's see what some of those one-eyed liars have had to say.

Lie #1: We Want to Become a Learning Organization.

This is a lie that many honest, well-intentioned people tell themselves. On some level, these liars really do believe that they want their organization to become an LO. Some of these folks want their companies to become LOs because they believe it will mean their organization embodies good values. Some want to become an LO because they sense that their organization is missing something—a compelling vision, openness to new ideas, or the ability to really examine ideas and make informed choices rather than merely reacting to the pressures of the day. Others seek the title of LO simply because it's the flavor of the month (at least in the 1990s, anyway).

The folks who tell this lie are the Candides of the world—the eternal optimists who think creating change is actually easy. However, most people have no idea what it means to really be an LO, including many supposed experts on the topic (see Lie #3). Even fewer know what it takes to become an LO—the incredible time, energy, and work it takes to bring about a significant set of sustainable changes in organizational culture and practice. Instead, what people have is the experience of having read a couple of good books and attended one or more engaging so-called transformational training programs.

> People have a warm, fuzzy idea that becoming an LO is a desirable thing; it is something they feel good about. At Innovation Associates, when prospective clients call and say, "We want to become a learning organization," we ask, "Why? Do you have any idea how much work that will be?"

Putting statements about organizational learning in the corporate vision statement won't make a company an LO. Making learning a critical success factor, putting in place a knowledge management (KM) system, or benchmarking best practices won't make a company an LO. Having a menu of training programs certainly won't make a company an LO; a company cannot become an LO through training alone. Learning about organizations will not make you an LO either. Bluntly put, there is no quick, easy way to become an LO, nor is there just one way to do so.

I have encountered several organizations striving to become a learning organization by focusing much of their effort and resources on KM. Here is the logic: "We keep reinventing the wheel around here. We are also losing experts and seasoned professionals through retirement, layoffs, and departures. We need to do something about all this vital knowledge that is not being shared across the organization and that is often walking out the door. We need to capture best practices and set up a KM system. If we get good at capturing and transferring knowledge around the company, we'll be a learning organization." Many organizations have invested millions of dollars in KM systems that are very sophisticated, user friendly, and impressive.

Unfortunately, the research has shown that almost no one uses them. What's the problem here? The problem is that although an effective system for knowledge capture is necessary (whether high tech or not) it is not sufficient to ensure knowledge will actually get shared and that any learning will happen. It appears that the individual and team learning barriers will defeat the most well-intentioned KM system. It is the human software—mindsets and mental models—and not the computer software that is the real impediment to sharing best practices and learning.

Becoming an LO may be something that a business never totally achieves. It is a journey, not a destination. Organizational learning is about a way of being and a way of approaching organizational issues more than it is about reaching some definable end state called a learning organization.

A word to the wise: Instituting any major change in an organization, including creating a culture of learning, is hard work. Every client

I have worked with in a major change initiative (and I have heard many other change consultants say the same thing) has, less than halfway through the process, sighed deeply and said, "If I had known how hard this was going to be, I don't know if I would have started it." It's tough work.

Rather than being Candide's imagined journey, creating any major change is more reminiscent of the cartoon character Pogo Possum, or the tortoise of Aesop's fable fame, or even President John F. Kennedy Jr.'s inaugural address.

Pogo Possum

Real systems change can occur only when a critical mass of people, including those at the top, come to the realization, as Pogo did, that "We have met the enemy, and he is us" (Kelly, 1972). We, together, have created our organizational reality, and we, together—and only together—can change it. Truly creating a learning culture involves "wrestling with Pogo"—changing the parts of your organization, including the parts that are deeply embedded, that keep your organization from being the kind of organization it wants to be (Ober, 1996). Achieving this realization is not the end of the journey; it is only the major first step. As Sir Winston Churchill described the United States' entry into World War II, "We cannot say that this is the end. We cannot even say that it is the beginning of the end, but we can say that it is the end of the beginning!" When a critical mass of individuals in the organization look in the mirror and say, "I have to change," the real work can start.

The Tortoise

Sustaining the learning journey will take a much longer time and a much greater investment of energy than most organizations are willing to make. The learning journey proceeds at a pace more akin to a tortoise's than a hare's. Becoming an LO involves aligning changes at multiple levels (individual, group, team, departmental, divisional, organizational, and marketwide). It involves changes in "hard stuff" (policies, procedures, structures, metrics) and "soft stuff" (the ways people relate, have conversations, work in teams, and think).

The moral of Aesop's fable, "Slow and steady wins the race," describes a process not unlike the flywheel envisioned by Jim Collins (2001): "No matter how dramatic the end result, the good-to-great transformations never happened in one fell swoop. There was no single defining action, no grand program, no one killer innovation, no solitary lucky break, and no miracle moment. Rather, the process resembled relentlessly pushing a giant heavy flywheel in one direction, turn upon turn, building momentum until a point of breakthrough and beyond." Often, I tell my clients, "The set of people and ideas that actually prevail in an organization are those that, like the turtle, can outlast the others!"

President John F. Kennedy, Jr.

Becoming an LO is not unlike how JFK, in his inaugural address, described the work of creating a peaceful world as a "a long, cold twilight struggle." It takes lots of time, hard work, and equal doses of hard realism and vibrant energy: "We may not achieve these things in the first 100 days, or in the first 1,000 days, or in our lifetimes in this planet, but let us begin!" Such is the commitment required to create any significant organizational change.

Instilling organizational learning often starts with a small group and spreads out over time. Many cases of major change in organizations involved small groups that made major strides in their own learning before the rest of the organization did. When these learners begin to innovate, however, they make other people anxious and envious, so the organization's antibodies reject them. They sometimes have to go underground to sustain the effort.

As Edgar Schein (1999) cautions, "Unless top leaders become learners themselves—unless they can acknowledge their own vulnerabilities and uncertainties—then transformational learning will never take place." For senior executives, acknowledging vulnerability can be very difficult. Doing so runs counter to everything that got them where they are today, and many executives are under tremendous pressure not to appear vulnerable and not to change.

One executive team I worked with used a business model developed during the 1920s and 1930s when it proved very effective. The team still recounts stories about their turn-of-the-last-century founders at almost every major meeting. Unfortunately, that business model is very ineffective for today's marketplace; the company has been losing money for the last 30 years. Despite this data, the senior executives continually fail to see their real situation: Their business model is outmoded, they're fueling the problem, and they need to change. They are under tremendous institutional pressures—massive holdings, huge retirement programs, unions, and the burden of the company's national reputation—to maintain the company's image and claim success. "Not on my watch" has become the organization's mantra in response to the need for acknowledging failure and making deep changes. Until tariffs are lifted and tremendous pressure comes to bear for change, this executive team never will be able to really learn. Ultimately, if the people at the top of the house, the major culture carriers and creators, are not able to practice and model a way of being that embodies learning, the organization cannot embody learning either.

A final comment about Lie #1: All of the above statements are about becoming an LO and are, as such, lies. They are lies because the phrase "becoming a learning organization" offers a false premise; it is not a useful way to frame, converse about, or work this set of issues. In fact, framing the concept of an LO in this way is an impediment. Proceeding in this way will, in all likelihood, result in expenditures of energy, time, money, and other resources that will not yield a return sufficient to justify the investment. Put bluntly, framing the work in this way will probably lead to failure.

Lie #2: Establishing LO Initiatives and Programs Makes a Learning Organization.

This is a lie many well-intentioned leaders and professionals within organizations tell themselves. It is also a lie many consultants and trainers, some with good intentions and some not, tell prospective clients. However, developing a separate initiative aimed at creating an LO can be dangerous and counterproductive.

One company made becoming an LO a key component of their corporate vision and strategy. The company paid a consulting firm thousands of dollars to administer an elaborate survey throughout the organization. The consultant recommended to the client that they produce a videotape based on a children's story about wolves and sheep as a way to communicate what an LO was about. Actors were hired and a video was produced to be shown throughout the entire engineering organization to get everyone involved. The effort came to a screeching halt when division heads said, "If we don't get rid of those stupid tapes, we're not going to touch this learning organization stuff." This initial effort set the LO work back about a year.

Becoming an LO really is about using LO approaches, methods, tools, and ways of being that can help your company become the kind of organization you want it to be. It is about focusing on business results and learning the things you need to learn to achieve them.

To paraphrase Edgar Schein (1999), an organization exists to achieve certain things and to deliver given products and services successfully in its environment. Making organizational culture changes that do not support that basic purpose makes no sense. Never start with the idea of making a culture change (for example, becoming an LO). Always start with the real business issues the organization is facing. Then ask, "Will LO approaches help us address these issues?"

The real work of the learning organization is about clarifying where you want to go as a company, being brutally honest about where you really are at present, and doing the hard work it takes to bridge the gap. LO approaches—systems thinking, building shared vision, team learning, mental models, personal mastery, and related approaches—are means to help you get there more effectively and more authentically. There is no one set of steps, no one path that will make you an LO. In fact, the journey often looks very different for different kinds of organizations because the focus needs to be on learning about the work and how to do the work better. As the content of the work varies, so, often, does the content of the learning.

Furthermore, unless an organization has a compelling business imperative that can be supported explicitly by LO approaches, they will not make the investment necessary to sustain organizational learning. They may start big. They may engage in lots of activities, use lots of resources, and spend plenty of money at the LO altar, but, without a compelling business imperative, they will not make the long-term commitment and create a new way of being. The reason they won't persevere is not that they are bad people or because they are lazy. They simply won't do it because they can't do it. Business forces, the forces of the real work, will systemically push them to focus their energy on doing that work rather than on engaging in standalone LO initiatives. No matter how much you strongly recommend, prod, or cajole, many client organizations will not accept the fact that unless they have a compelling business imperative, the learning organization work simply won't take. Unless the real work and LO are transparently intertwined, organizational learning won't happen. There is a fundamental paradox in LO work: If becoming an LO is in the foreground and the real work of the organization is in the background, efforts to incorporate organizational learning will not work. To succeed, LO work must be in the background.

Lie #3: We Know How to Help You Become a Learning Organization.

This lie is told by many well-intentioned professionals—and by some who are not so well intentioned. In the last 15 years, especially during the height of the LO movement in the 1990s, nearly every management consulting firm—solo shops, boutiques, the Big Eight, the crème de la crème—has jumped on the LO bandwagon and proclaimed, "We can help you. We know how to do it." Most of these firms know the lingo. Some of them even have a good handle on the content they lifted from Innovation Associates, Peter Senge (author of *The Fifth Discipline,* 1994), and other LO pioneers. Very few of them, however, approach the work at the level of being.

Furthermore, big consulting is not always a game about learning or even about helping client organizations be better companies. Because of the tremendous pressure to perform, it is sometimes a game about money and power—get the big contracts, write the best sellers, garner the most powerful clients. At times, less comfortable learning issues are swept under the rug so that the relationship and the flow of big checks can be maintained. Again, it is not that the people who engage in this lie are bad people or that they do it intentionally. They do it because they are under tremendous pressure to perform, deliver huge contracts, become partners, and stay ahead of the competition.

Therefore, it is very hard for companies to know where to get effective help and to know if they are getting the real thing. Many folks may be calling themselves LO consultants because the LO concept is popular and because it sells, not because they have mastered the art.

To be successful at really learning in the LO field, an organization cannot ultimately rely on external consultants. Good consultants can help get an organization started and help them learn about their work, but to be successful over the long term, organizations have to develop internal capability. Learning organization work is not something that can be done for you or to you; it is something you have to do for yourself. So, watch out. Anyone who leads with "We can help you become a learning organization," probably can't. Consultants cannot help you very much if they don't challenge you to

➤ focus on your business rather than on becoming an LO
➤ clearly identify your compelling business imperatives
➤ be brutally honest about where you are
➤ do the hard work it will take to bridge the gap
➤ learn the things it takes to do your real business more effectively.

Beware of any LO consultant who does not challenge you to do this hard work and, only if and as appropriate, use LO approaches as aides. There is plenty of snake oil out there but precious little real medicine.

Lie #4: Organizational Learning Is About Organizations Learning.

This lie is one that most people in the LO field tell (passively if not actively) because they haven't done the hard work to figure out what learning at the organizational level really is. To find out if this statement is a lie, read some of the LO literature and watch the activities at LO conferences. Most of the work described as organizational learning is not about learning at the organizational level.

What is labeled as organizational learning is primarily about individual learning and secondarily about groups and teams learning. There is actually scant focus on helping the entire organization learn. There is an emphasis on knowledge, technologies, and approaches that further learning at the individual level. We have a good deal of knowledge about learning at the group and team level, but there's much less—some would say almost nothing—about learning on an organization-wide level.

The assumption seems to be that if many individuals and teams in an organization learn, that learning will automatically roll up into organizational learning with the entire organization as the unit of change. But, is that true? Does enough individual and team learning automatically create organizational learning? I'm not sure the answer is known. What does it mean to learn at the organizational level? How does an organization learn? How is an organization that is learning different from one that is not learning? How is an organization different after it has learned than it was before? Perhaps it is incumbent on learning professionals to do one of two things: (1) create a model to represent how organizations learn, or (2) change the name "learning organization" to "organizations in which a lot of people learn."

What would learning at the level of the entire organization involve? The purpose of an organization is to deliver results, products, or services in its environment. Organizational learning is learning whereby the entire organization is the unit of change. Therefore,

Every organization has a more or less clearly articulated interacting set of procedures, structures, processes, operations, and conversations. The organization uses these to gather data about its environment, respond effectively, deliver its products and services, assess its success, adjust, and, thereby, continue to survive. This is called the organization's operational model. Learning at the organizational level is about the organization effectively adapting its operational model for survival.

When an organization stops effectively adapting its operational model to changing conditions, when it stops learning, it will eventually die—it will go the way of Digital Equipment Corporation, Data General, Arthur Andersen, and the myriad others that have disappeared into the elephant's graveyard. In contrast, an organization that learns will continually seek to understand and adapt its operational model to its changing environment so that it can continue to "live long and prosper," to borrow a phrase from Mr. Spock of *Star Trek* fame.

organizational learning is about increasing the entire organization's capacity to fulfill its purpose more effectively. Organizational learning is about adapting the organization's *operational model.*

Overcoming the Lies With Truth

To be fair, there is exciting work occurring out there that broadens the unit of change. Some practitioners are supporting learning communities that run throughout organizations. Other practitioners do open-space work that aims to fundamentally change an entire system. These practices have not primarily grown out of the organizational learning community, but they are very hopeful trends with which the LO practice should ally.

The Lie	The Truth
We want to become a learning organization.	Most people have no idea what it means to really be an LO, including many supposed experts on the topic. Even fewer know what it takes to become an LO—the incredible time, energy, and work it takes to bring about a significant set of sustainable changes in organizational culture and practice.
Establishing LO initiatives and programs makes a learning organization.	Becoming an LO really is about using LO approaches, methods, tools, and ways of being that can help your company become the kind of organization you want it to be. It is about focusing on business results and learning the things you need to learn to achieve them.
We know how to help you become a learning organization.	To be successful in the LO field, an organization cannot ultimately rely on external consultants. Good consultants can help get an organization started and help them learn about their work, but to be successful over the long term, organizations have to develop internal capability.
Organizational learning is about organizations learning.	What is labeled as organizational learning is primarily about individual learning and secondarily about groups and team learning. Organizational learning is learning whereby the entire organization is the unit of change. Therefore, organizational learning is about increasing the entire organization's capacity to fulfill its purpose more effectively.

References

Collins, J. (2001). *Good to Great: Why Some Companies Make the Leap...and Others Don't.* New York: HarperCollins.

Kelly, W. (1972). *Pogo: We Have Met the Enemy and He Is Us.* New York: Simon and Schuster.

Ober, S. (1996). *Wrestling Pogo—Toward a Model of Organizational Learning.* Cambridge, MA: Arthur D. Little.

Schein, E. (1999). *The Corporate Culture Survival Guide.* San Francisco: Jossey-Bass.

Senge, P.M. (1994). *The Fifth Discipline: The Art and Practice of the Learning Organization.* New York: Currency/Random House.

Lies About Research

David E. Stone

The Big Lie: If You Review Enough Research, You Will Find the Answers You Need

If you have the responsibility for making important decisions about learning and performance improvement in your company, you probably don't have the time to conduct formal research on learning and performance improvement. You must rely on the work of others to guide your decisions. You might think that if you review enough of the research available on learning and performance improvement and the products and services based on that research that you will find the guidance that you seek.

Unfortunately, such is not the case.

A review of the published research may reveal contradictory studies, inconclusive results, or conflicting theories about how people learn. This chapter offers some insights that will help you identify research that can help, rather than hinder, your efforts to find valid theories and good products and services to support your efforts.

In 1980, I had the opportunity to work in a company that had won the right to take a National Science Foundation (NSF) project and market it as a turnkey hardware and software system for the design, delivery, and deployment of learning and performance support

> Research can be interpreted in many ways. There is no guarantee that reviewing all the research on any topic will give you the answers you need to select a procedure or service. The fact is that there are poor studies, incorrect figures, and sloppy research that can cause you to stumble as you are investigating learning programs. This chapter is devoted to a sound approach to evaluating the validity and applicability of research to support learning and performance improvement.

content. One of my first tasks in that job was to review the research on the effectiveness of computer-based instruction and assemble the results into a report to support the sale of that system.

In those days, such systems cost hundreds of thousands or even millions of dollars, and it was a challenge to make the case for spending that kind of money. The studies that I could find were primarily designed to show that computer-based instruction was a more effective method than other means of instruction. The studies didn't attempt to explain in any depth what was behind these findings or relate them to any particular theory of learning and performance improvement.

The studies I analyzed simply concluded that method *A* was better than method *B*. Method *A* led to better retention, better performance, and faster completion times than method *B*. My compilation of the results was widely used by the company to support its sales efforts. I suspect, however, that those results were not a significant factor in many buying decisions.

As it happens, many of the customers for this particular product chose it because it was the low-cost option. Back then, it cost $80,000 an hour to put a student pilot in a military flight simulator. It was quite easy to justify the cost of any computer program that could provide aircraft instrument and procedure training and reduce significantly the costly flight-simulation hours.

Now it is no longer necessary to justify the use of computers for learning and performance improvement. Industry leaders need to provide solutions for business problems in the global enterprise and decision makers require an understanding of performance improvement technology that goes deeper than "Is it a good thing or a bad thing?" Perhaps I can offer some thoughts about what to consider when someone comes to your office to tell you about a new product or service that "research proves" will solve all your problems.

The Fine Line Between Fact and Theory

Are theories really necessary? We live at a time when the very idea of science is under attack not only in remote parts of the world, but also in our own country. Arguments rage over what is fact and what is theory. For those who are in that struggle, it might be worthwhile to read *The Structure of Scientific Revolutions* (Kuhn, 1996), which provides a historical context for understanding the role of science in our society.

"There is nothing so practical as a good theory." This statement by Kurt Lewin (1951, p. 169) may sound a bit odd to people who tend to think of scientific theory as far removed from the practical realities of everyday life. Yet the statement is true on several levels.

First, good theories in science generate testable hypotheses so that the theories that have been put forward by researchers can be evaluated objectively by the scientific community. Theories that have great explanatory power and are substantiated by experimental research are taught in our educational system and form the core of our understanding of the natural world around us.

Second, theoretical frameworks guide people through the practical realities of everyday life. For example, the scientific theory of disease has led to the development of medicines that cure diseases, such as polio, that used to take a terrible toll of human life around the world. Disease theory has led to effective methods of sanitation, water treatment, and food preparation.

One might reasonably wonder how all this pertains to educational practice or efforts to improve learning and performance in the workplace. A foundation for effective learning and instruction using technology does exist. There are theories of learning, and these theories are supported by rigorous scientific research. A good understanding of these theories and the related research along with practical experience in various methods and technologies used to improve learning and performance are at the core of the educational preparation of many professionals in the field of learning and performance improvement.

Professionals who have responsibility for learning and performance improvement have the daily challenge to make decisions based on evaluations of products and services that are surrounded by claims that are often said to be based on solid research. They may draw on their professional preparation and a good knowledge of theory and research, but their decisions often rely on claims that are suspect.

Harvard psychologist Jerome Bruner (1966) asserts that "...learning is an active process in which learners construct new ideas or concepts based upon their current/past knowledge. The learner selects and transforms information, constructs hypotheses, and makes decisions, relying on a cognitive structure to do so. Cognitive structure (schema, mental models) provides meaning and organization to experiences and allows the individual 'to go beyond the information given.'"

Questions to Ask About Research

Who did the research? Who paid for it? Just as you consider the source when hearing office gossip, you should consider the source when evaluating research. Was the work done by an independent organization such as a university with a long history of doing solid research or was it done by a research institute created to advance the agenda of a particular industry or company?

Some of the best research on online learning was done years ago and funded by the National Science Foundation under the PLATO project. This research is housed within the university library system at the University of Illinois. The U.S. government has, over the years, funded some excellent university-based research on a wide range of topics ranging from the applications of artificial intelligence to computer-based instruction to how to design information delivered by electronic performance support systems. The Office of Naval Research and the Army Research Institute for the Behavioral and Social Sciences have funded much of this work.

Research on learning and performance improvement is being conducted all over the world. However, much of that research is still based in American universities. A survey conducted by *The Times* of London revealed that U.S. institutions occupied seven of the top 10 places (Halpin, 2004). "Harvard, which boasts an endowment of nearly $23 billion (£12.7 billion), was first in the list produced by *The Times Higher Education Supplement* (THES)."According to the article, "Cambridge, Massachusetts, however, can lay claim to being the world's most intellectual city, as home to Harvard and to the Massachusetts Institute of Technology, which was ranked at No. 3." Harvard has a unique academic culture that is fiercely independent and that, for a variety of reasons (including great wealth), is free to focus on both basic and applied research without many of the constraints found in other universities.

Some readers may recall the film *The Fugitive* with Harrison Ford as the doctor wrongly accused of murdering his wife. In this film, viewers discover that a multibillion-dollar pharmaceutical company has worked with a hospital and medical school to falsify the results of research on a new drug and thereby make billions in profits. Universities rightly fear the potentially corrupting influence of the profit motive and sometimes avoid collaboration with industry out of that fear. Indeed, safeguards are needed to ensure that university-based research avoids undue influence—by those with the funds and the motivation—to ensure that research results are accurate.

My own research on learning and performance improvement is now primarily based at MIT where I am a research fellow and a part of the augmented reality (AR) group headed by my friend and colleague Eric Klopfer. Although Klopfer's group at MIT has focused on medical applications for AR, we have recently found several industrial applications for this technology that include improving driver safety and package delivery systems.

MIT has more than its fair share of Nobel Laureate scientists, mathematicians, and engineers. Some people believe that MIT is the greatest technical university in the world. Anyone who has seen the movie *Good Will Hunting* has caught a glimpse of the exciting achievement at this stellar institution. However, MIT also has organizational structures that are designed to bridge the gap between pure theoretical research and the needs of industry. Such organizations as the MIT Center for eBusiness and the Media Lab are staffed with leaders and managers who understand not only the world of the university but also the world of global business. This matters because this layer of organization along with competent research management makes the process of industry–university collaboration straightforward and highly productive. Global companies can count on MIT to be not only experts in theory and basic research, but also highly competent in taking advances in theory and basic research and implementing them in ways that solve business problems.

For example, the Media Lab is well known for inventing digital photography and other advances in technology and for requiring that researchers build working prototypes that implement these advances in ways that demonstrate their practical utility.

MIT has put in place agreements between global companies and the Center for eBusiness that ensure that the research meets both the needs of the industry sponsor and the global mission of the university. MIT is also a world leader in making the benefits of technology-based learning and performance support available to everyone.

My advice to those in the learning industry who have a need to address near-term business problems is to look for organizations that have a culture that supports unbiased research but are staffed with professionals that can bridge the gap between the goals of a university and the needs of business.

Has the Research Been Published in a Refereed Journal?

Was the research published in a refereed or peer-reviewed journal? Good research is subject to peer review by recognized experts in a field before it is published in a journal. Did this research pass this test, or was it just published in a trade journal? There are many well-respected scientific journals that publish research with implications for those responsible for learning and performance improvement. One such journal is *Human Performance,* described thus by its publisher:

> This journal publishes research investigating the nature of performance in the workplace and in applied settings and offers a rich variety of information going beyond the study of traditional job behavior. Dedicated to presenting original research, theory, and measurement methods, the journal investigates individual

and team performance factors that influence work effectiveness. *Human Performance* is a respected forum for behavioral scientists interested in variables that motivate and promote high-level human performance, particularly in occupational settings. The journal seeks to identify and stimulate more relevant research, communication, and theory concerning human capabilities and effectiveness. It serves as a valuable intellectual link between such disciplines as industrial-organizational psychology, individual differences, work physiology, environmental medicine and safety, human resource management, and human factors.

There are also organizations, such as Society for Applied Learning Technology (www.salt.org), that have a long history of conducting conferences and publishing journals that are known for both their respect for the scientific method and for the deep experience of the organization's leadership.

On Whom Can You Rely for Professional Advice?

Many of us have been to conferences that are essentially tradeshows that lack the professionalism and perspective that only comes with years of experience with learning and performance improvement technology. Although it is always interesting to talk to vendors, it is perhaps more important to talk to your peers who face similar challenges because they can share their experiences with you. This kind of thinking led me to create the e-Learning Crew (ELC) (http://blogs.law .harvard.edu/ethics) to bring together thought leaders from United Parcel Service, General Electric, Analog Devices, Wyeth, Bayer Medical Systems, Dade Behring, Randstad, Harvard, MIT, and other organizations on a monthly basis to share their knowledge and experience.

> Don't even think about buying a product or implementing a solution without seeking the advice and experience of your peers. Don't even think about accepting the results of research that has not been peer reviewed.

What Is the Theoretical Foundation for the Research?

Is the research related to a particular theory of learning and, if so, do the results advance the understanding of how people learn? There are many theories with respect to learning and performance improvement. In fact, there may be too many theories. Remember Lewin's words: "There is nothing so practical as a good theory." At present, learning professionals are hindered by the lack of a comprehensive theory of learning and performance improvement that addresses video-game-style simulations, radio-style Podcasts, community-building internal blogs, and support systems delivered on Blackberries and other personal digital assistants (PDAs). Despite this gap, the research should relate easily to one or more established theories of learning and performance improvement.

Some might ask why that should matter. Whatever tools or technologies you may be considering in your efforts to improve learning and performance across the enterprise, you will surely need to consider the context in which they will be used, how to best implement them to achieve your business goals, and how to measure and evaluate your solution in business terms. A theoretical framework can provide the conceptual structure needed to do all of these things. Without one, you may miss opportunities to take the most advantage of your investment.

Perhaps you don't subscribe to any particular theory at all. If you aren't sure which theoretical approach would be best for your situation, perhaps you should devote some time to considering several and seeing how they have been successfully applied to challenges in learning and performance improvement. If you find some examples that seem to be close to your situation, you could try one or two on a small scale to see how they might add value to your efforts.

Was the Research Done to Sell a Product or to Answer Deeper Questions?

Is the research focused on a single product or is it designed to advance knowledge of learning and performance improvement in a way that is applicable to a class of products? Research on a single product tends to be motivated by commercial concerns rather than expanding the knowledge and understanding of a particular aspect of learning and, because products come and go, may be of limited value.

Product-based case studies are always interesting and often used to support claims for products. "Use of product X resulted in an 82 percent reduction in compliance training cycle time for a major insurance company," says a leading vendor of enterprise software. Who am I to question that claim? In fact, I don't question it at all. I believe that this particular product helped the insurance company achieve the results it reported.

However, I am interested in those particular features of the product and those variables that led to this result. For example, what is being compared to what? That is, how did the insurance company conduct compliance training before they started to use the leading vendor's enterprise software? Did they use any technology at all or was the training delivered by instructors with the results kept manually? Based on my reading of the study, the dramatic results reported through use of the vendor's enterprise software can be attributed to the fact that the new compliance training was delivered as e-learning instead of traditional classroom instruction.

Whether similar results could have been obtained by using any of the many other software systems with similar features to the vendor's enterprise software is an open question. Stating the results as an 82 percent reduction in compliance training cycle time certainly creates the impression of a dramatic improvement, but I am not convinced that this particular product is the only one that could achieve similar results in these circumstances.

Be skeptical of research claims made about products, but be sure to read the research and ask those who conducted it questions designed to elicit the similarities and differences between the conditions in the study and your circumstances. If you decide to license and implement the product, consider engaging the researchers as consultants to facilitate your implementation.

Was the Research Done in a Real-World Setting?

Do the conditions under which the study was conducted approximate those of your organization's working environment? Much university-based research is conducted using a population of college students. The characteristics of such a population may differ significantly from that of the global workforce in your company. The controlled environment that was used in the university psychology lab or usability lab may also differ in significant ways from the environment where your employees will actually use the application. Bear in mind that if this is the case, the results of the research may not be fully applicable to your situation.

A major software vendor uses case studies to illustrate how organizations can benefit from the use of its products:

> "In 2000, [a university] created a trial portal based on [software company product] with 1,000 students and 30 members of staff as users. The feedback from this project was incredibly encouraging, so the university started to look at the market for ways to expand the portal university-wide. It considered building a portal from scratch and off-the-shelf products, but the former would have been time consuming and costly, and the latter might have restricted functionality and future scope. [The university] decided on a building block approach to create a best-of-breed system with the right price, the right development effort, and the right features. [The software company product] was selected to complement the university's existing skill set and deliver the capabilities it required."

The questions to consider in reading this case study are "How similar or different are the circumstances of this case study to the challenges I face in my organization?" and, if the circumstances are similar, "How can I achieve similar results given the specific differences in my situation?"

If you are seriously contemplating licensing and implementing a software or hardware product enterprisewide and if your careful analysis of your needs has led you to research a particular product, do so. However, be sure to take the time to visit companies similar to yours that have successfully implemented the product. Be sure to ask hard questions about the problems encountered in the pilot phase of other companies' implementations. (Don't believe vendors if they say that there were none.)

What Was the Research Methodology?

How was the research conducted? Was there a formal research design with appropriate statistical analysis of the results or was this a case of someone trying out a new product with a small sample of people in a special set of circumstances that might not be relevant to your situation? Has the research been replicated?

As discussed, research in a university lab may not be fully applicable to your situation. It is also true that research that lacks a formal design and statistical analysis of the results may also not apply. Statistical analysis of results arrived at through a carefully designed experiment can determine whether the results achieved are the result of chance or are the result of the variable of interest. Without a controlled experiment with statistical analysis of the results, you can't know whether your results are just a chance occurrence.

The authors of the study of e-therapy described in the following abstract are to be commended for being forthright about its limitations:

This study explores the history and potential role for therapy delivered through e-learning. Problems with previous trials are discussed and the future role for blended therapy is examined. For purposes of this study the author created an online programme focusing on meta-therapy skills, i.e. a general problem-solving programme rather than a problem-specific approach. The programme content was based on established principles of cognitive therapy and is called "How to Think, Solve Problems and Make Decisions, Part 1." A pilot study using this programme was conducted in a nonclinical population using both blended learning and face-to-face contact. Only seven subjects were assessed due to time and resource constraints.

The study is subject to significant limitations. First, the number of participants does not allow for statistical analysis and results and conclusions are based on qualitative feedback rather than quantitative analysis. Second, the content of both the face-to-face interviews and the online content were limited to what could be achieved over a time span of 3 weeks. Conclusions were based on a combination of the literature review, feedback given by participants in the study, and the assessment of the author.

The conclusions reached are (1) that the potential for e-therapy would not be realized through a simple translation of existing therapy into online delivery. Instead e-therapy offers the potential to develop an entirely new form of therapy that, when compared to traditional face-to-face treatment, would differ in the psychological effects and outcomes for the users. (2) Existing cultural barriers to the development of online therapy arise because of the misperception that it would replace "therapy by therapist" with "therapy by computer," thereby lacking the powerful component of empathy and human contact. However, the potential for e-therapy would not be about replacing psychologists but could lead to their expanded role bringing about more effective delivery and new treatment methods.

Studies such as these can be very helpful in that they may help redefine the questions under study and define key variables that can be tested once resources are made available. To follow up on what appear to be promising results, more rigorous studies that meet the requirements for generalizing the findings to a larger population may need to be conducted.

In this case, it appears that e-therapy has the promise of expanding the role of psychologists in bringing more effective delivery and new treatment methods. However, it would be inappropriate to immediately make sweeping generalizations about e-therapy based on this study alone. Has the research been replicated? In some cases, results of research may be fabricated, although it seems likely that failure to replicate results is most often the result of a desire by researchers to break new ground rather than simply confirm someone else's results. Whether this is the case, if the research presented to you in support of a new product or technology has not been replicated it may be too soon for you to decide to adopt it in your organization. Even if the research is published in a refereed journal, if the research has not been replicated at another location by another team of researchers you don't really know if the results can be counted on.

Better still, find other companies that have the same profile as yours and visit them to learn of their experience with the technology or product that you are considering. If you are fortunate, they will share what surprised them, what took longer than expected, what broke their budget, what they learned about implementing and gaining acceptance for the innovation within their organization, and finally, whether it was really worth it.

Being the first to implement a new product or technology may be exciting, but there is an argument to be made for being just behind the bleeding edge of research and development. Sometimes it makes sense to let others take those first uncertain steps into new territory so that you can benefit from their mistakes without having the costs associated with being a pioneer. I say that because I've had the experience in my career of being 20 or 30 years too early in adopting new technology and methods of instruction. There is, however, something to be said for having 30 years of experience in a "new" field. Larry Israelite (the editor of this book) and I published articles on new learning and performance improvement models in the 1980s that are only now being widely adopted.

In 1982, I led a project funded by the U.S. Army Institute for the Behavioral and Social Sciences that created an electronic performance support system (EPSS) for maintaining tanks. I remember demonstrating that technology at the Army Tank Command in Warren, Michigan, in the summer of that year. I had actually built my first EPSS while a graduate student at Cornell University in 1976, but this one used procedural text and graphics with hypertext and troubleshooting logic that were many years before their time.

Now, of course, such hardware and software systems are common and they fit in the palm of your hand while linking you wirelessly to vast networks. They are used to deliver reference information to medical personnel, provide troubleshooting logic to repair technicians, and much more. For those that wonder what is coming next, I suggest reading *The Singularity Is Near* (Kurzweil, 2005). The world of 2015 will be very, very different from our world today. You won't need to wait as long as I have for dreams to come true.

The world of 2015 will be very, very different from our world today. You won't need to wait as long as I have for dreams to come true.

Overcoming the Lies With Truth

Here is a list of things to consider when confronted with research used to support product claims:

Question to Ask	Rationale
Who did the research?	The research is more credible if done by an organization that doesn't have a stake in the outcome but does have a track record of doing good research that is respected as meeting scientific standards.
Who paid for the research?	Although good, independent research can be funded by any organization, be suspicious of research funded to support a particular agenda.
Has the research been published in a refereed journal?	By subjecting research findings to careful scrutiny in terms of study design and rigorous statistical analysis, one can be assured that the study's findings are likely to be valid and reproducible.
Was the research done to sell a product or to answer deeper questions?	Because products come and go, research that answers more general questions about how a type of software product can be used is often more useful than answers about a specific product.
Was the research done in a real-world setting? Do the conditions under which the study was conducted approximate those of your organization's working environment?	Great research is done in laboratories, but it is vital that you find out if the results are generalizable to your environment.
Has the research been replicated?	If others have run similar studies and found similar results, it is more likely that these results are valid findings. Consider contacting others who have conducted similar studies to learn more about their findings.

If you keep these questions in mind when approaching the research phase of your program, you may avoid some common research pitfalls. It is important to remember that a careful and critical review of published research is more important than a comprehensive review of everything published on the topic of interest. You may never get the exact answer you are looking for. However, you may be able to gain new insights into the learning process and identify key considerations that will guide your search for the products and services that can best meet your organization's needs.

References

Bruner, J. (1966). *Toward a Theory of Instruction.* Cambridge, MA: Harvard University Press.

Halpin, T. (2004, November 4). "Britain Wins Eight Places in World List of 50 Best Universities." *The Times.* http://www.timesonline.co.uk /article/0,,2-1343642,00.html.

Kuhn, T. (1996). *The Structure of Scientific Revolutions.* Chicago: University of Chicago Press.

Kurzweil, R. (2005). *The Singularity Is Near: When Humans Transcend Biology.* New York: Penguin Group.

Lewin, K. (1951). *Field Theory in Social Science.* New York: Harper & Row.

Other Recommended Readings

Bruner, J. (1960). *The Process of Education.* Cambridge, MA: Harvard University Press.

Campbell, D.T., and J.C. Stanley. (1963). *Experimental and Quasi-Experimental Designs for Research.* New York: Houghton-Mifflin.

Stone, D.E., and L. Israelite. (1983). *A Hypertext Job Aid for Electronic Maintenance. Final Project Report.* Arlington, VA: U.S. Army Research Institute for the Behavioral and Social Sciences.

Stone, D.E., and C. Koskinen. (2002). *Planning and Design for High-Tech Web-Based Training.* New York: Artech House.

Stone, D.E., and J.C. Potter. (In press). *In Search of Perfect Performance.* New York: Auerbach Publications.

Final Thoughts: Some Truths About Learning

Larry Israelite

My goal for this book was to identify some of the challenges we face as learning professionals and to provide some simple approaches to dealing with them. I know they aren't all lies, although too often we become victims of creative marketing intended to sell products and services that will never achieve the promised results. Truth be known, this isn't much different from anything in life: Cars never achieve the gas mileage listed on the window sticker, nobody loses the weight promised by the latest and greatest diet book, and many products never see the end of their warranty periods. The point, of course, is that people have grown accustomed to living in a world in which the reality never lives up to the hype, and most have simply learned to accept this fact, both personally and professionally.

Although they focused on the lies associated with their respective topics, the experts who contributed to this effort based their work on the truth. Because the goal was to provide you with some tools to achieve success in the face of the challenges you face every day, it would be disingenuous for me not to spend at least some time focusing on that which we know to be true about some of the same topics. By doing so, perhaps I can restore some semblance of order to our somewhat confusing and often frustrating cosmos.

Learners Aren't the Only Ones Who Matter

The truth about learners is that often they are not the only constituency whose needs have to be satisfied when creating learning interventions. Although there is no doubt that we design a learning experience for its ultimate users, they are but one element of a complex web of interested parties whose needs and interests must be accounted for when creating a learning intervention.

For example, we are often asked to create programs (or other solutions) by business leaders who are trying to address specific business needs through learning, for example, to increase the profitability of each sale or reduce the length of calls to a service center. We are hired, essentially, to solve specific problems by creating a measurable change in learner performance. Sometimes the needs of clients conflict with the interests or desires of learners.

Many years ago, I was asked by a business unit leader to design a project management class with a significant emphasis on budgeting and forecasting. I complied with his request and designed several exercises intended to address this stated need. When the class ran, participants convinced the instructor that because they didn't do budgeting and forecasting, there was no need to spend much time on those subjects. Therefore, the instructor skipped them. Participants (learners) were happy because they didn't have to learn content they didn't want to learn, and the instructor was happy because his end-of-class evaluations were extremely high. Unfortunately, my client was angry. As he explained to me after the class ran, his employees were correct in saying that they didn't do budgeting and forecasting, which was why most of their projects were over budget and delivered late. Quite simply, the instructor had put the learners' needs above those of the project sponsor, and, therefore, the solution did not solve the problem he hired us to address.

There is no doubt that learner needs must be considered when creating learning solutions. Failure to do so will dramatically reduce the likelihood of success. So, too, will ignoring or paying insufficient attention to the needs of rest of the stakeholders, including the people who request learning solutions, pay for them, feel the effect of them (or lack thereof), and, yes, deliver them. You must consider everyone's needs, design solutions that address as many of them as you can, and be prepared to deal with the people whose needs you were unable to meet. If possible, be prepared to recommend options for meeting those needs in another way.

Content Isn't the Only Thing That Requires Good Design

As Mark Twain said, "Reports of my death have been greatly exaggerated." This one sums up in a single sentence the response of instructional designers who are tired of hearing that we are part of a dead or, at least, irrelevant profession. Instructional designers are as necessary now as they ever were, and one might even argue that with the availability of increasingly varied and complex delivery media, that they might be needed more than ever. I would, however, be remiss if I did not point out that instructional design isn't the only profession that has fallen victim to the "no design is necessary" mantra. In such cases, some new tool or technology almost always was to blame.

My wife was a graphic designer. She spent several years in school and close to 20 years refining her art. In the late 1980s, desktop publishing software began to make its way to the desks of secretaries, administrative assistants, and many others in their places of work. I'm sure you are familiar with the result: Badly designed and generally awful newsletters, presentations, and brochures were popping out of computers everywhere. It suddenly became much more difficult for my wife and graphic designers everywhere to find work, and if they did find it, their salaries or hourly consulting rates were low. As you might have guessed, people started saying that graphic design, as a profession, was dead, all because of the creation of a new category of tools.

Those people were wrong. Over time, it became obvious that these new graphics tools were necessary, but not sufficient. There is an art and a science to well-designed graphics; font selection matters and the shape, size, and placement of graphic elements—even the amount of white space—affect understanding and impact. Over time, graphic designers regained their rightful place on production teams, along with other professionals whose skills and talents were alleged to be embodied in software tools. The fact is that instructional design, graphic design, user interface design, code design, and other forms of design are critical to the creation of effective learning products. Never assume that new tools or technologies can replace the talent of professional designers. They can't! What they will do is allow you to increase the impact those resources can have on your projects. That is nothing to sneeze at.

A Job in Learning Does Not a Learning Professional Make

Training organizations are a corporate melting pot. People from all walks of corporate life, from a variety of professional and educational background and interests, and with practically any organizational affiliation can wind up in a training organization. In some cases, this happens voluntarily, and other times it happens by accident, by leadership fiat, or for any number of other reasons, most of which are beyond our control. Regardless, people wake up one morning and discover they are trainers, learning consultants, or program developers. The question this raises is whether our profession is well served by so willingly accepting what I refer to as accidental professionals.

There is little doubt that learning organizations that comprise people from a variety of backgrounds are better positioned to provide meaningful solutions to their customers. Clearly, good reasons exist, for example, for having successful sales people teach new-hire sales training programs, the least of which is instant credibility and rapport with the audience. But, isn't having expertise in the art and science of teaching equally as important as having subject matter expertise? Shouldn't these trainers understand (and respect) the learning theories and design strategies on which the programs they deliver are based? Wouldn't they be more effective if they knew about and could apply a variety of facilitation techniques based on the learning styles and personal characteristics of the people in their classes? Wouldn't we all be in a better position to deliver real value to our stakeholders if we insisted that all the people who come to us from other organizations have a similar level of expertise in our profession as they have in their own?

We have far too many accidental professionals in our midst. They meander into careers in learning but won't (or don't) acknowledge that we are, in fact, a collection of professions. And, far too often, we don't require them to become proficient at, if not experts in, our various professional disciplines. We allow them, our clients, our corporate leaders, and even our colleagues to perpetrate the myth that anyone can do our jobs. By so doing, we allow ourselves to be underappreciated and undervalued. We need to make learning an intentional profession that people choose because they want to become experts in the disciplines we practice and then derive personal and professional satisfaction by doing the work we do.

Certainly, our profession benefits greatly from diversity. We have all learned a great deal from the businesspeople with whom we have worked. Nevertheless, what is needed is a policy of professional reciprocity. If I went to work in a business unit as a consultant, I would be expected to become an expert in the products and services on which I was consulting, to understand and to be able to apply the consulting process used in that organization, and, finally, to have specific expertise in the art and science of consulting itself. It is reasonable to expect that businesspeople who come to work in our organizations should become experts in what we do. Not having that expectation sends a clear signal that even we are not convinced that we have unique skills and capabilities that are necessary for doing the work we do.

Those of us who have chosen careers in learning need to look in the mirror a little more frequently. We need to ask ourselves some hard questions from time to time to make sure that we are doing everything we can do to deliver value to our clients:

➤ Do we think and act like businesspeople whose main goals are the creation of products and services that deliver meaningful, measurable value to our clients, subject to the same constraints under which all businesses operate?

➤ Do we hold ourselves accountable for things (whatever they are) that our clients believe have value to them?

➤ Do we continually seek out ways to become more crucial to the success of the businesses we support?

> ➤ Do we remain current with the research and development associated with our professional disciplines so that we can offer an ever-increasing array of options for addressing learning needs?
> ➤ Do we collaborate with consultants and vendors in a way that ensures mutual success?
> ➤ Can we say with a high degree of certainty that our organizations are better off because we exist and that they would achieve less were we to disappear?

We must strive to answer yes to all of those questions, and, if we can't, we must figure out what we have to change so we can. Otherwise, at least two things will happen: (1) We will perpetuate the myth (lie) that it is OK for us to be an accidental profession and that anyone can do the work that we do because there is no special knowledge, skill, or competence required to do it; or (2) we will become yet another over-head organization whose value is misunderstood and whose very existence is called into question.

It doesn't matter if we call ourselves training, learning, or performance consultants; instructional designers or developers; e-learning programmers, authors, or coders; or directors, vice presidents, or chiefs. It doesn't matter how we are organized or if we are part of human resources, a business unit, or some other function. It really doesn't matter if we are internal, external, consultants, suppliers, outsourcers, or vendors. What does matter is that we are experts at what we do, regardless of the path we took to the profession of learning, that we accept responsibility for the results we achieve, and that we make meaningful, measurable contributions to the businesses we support. Then, and only then, will we have a chance to achieve the recognition we want and the respect we deserve.

We Will Never Succeed if We Think About Solutions First

Whenever I work with clients, I spend a great deal of time trying to help them clarify their goals. I ask them repeatedly to explain to me in concise terms exactly what it is they are hoping to achieve as a result of the project we are about to begin. This is hard work and the conversations are often difficult because most of us just want to talk about solutions.

What does matter is that we are experts at what we do, regardless of the path we took to the profession of learning, that we accept responsibility for the results we achieve, and that we make meaningful, measurable contributions to the businesses we support. Then, and only then, will we have a chance to achieve the recognition we want and the respect we deserve.

As anyone who knows me will corroborate, I can be quite stubborn, and I am very stubborn about this. I have yet to regret taking this approach, and in those situations when I haven't been as diligent about it as I should have been, the projects have taken longer, cost more, been more difficult, or didn't achieve the desired results. Only after the goals are clear do I feel comfortable moving on to the rest of the engagement. Interestingly, several clients have told me recently that they, too, now think about goals first and that this way of thinking has really helped them to become more effective and efficient in their own work.

When creating learning solutions, goals are the first but not the only thing about which we must be clear. We also need to have a deep and explicit understanding of audience characteristics, stakeholder needs, learning outcomes, content, learning environment, and other similar factors to define a solution that will maximize the likelihood that the learning objectives will be achieved. In some ways, this is like plotting the route for a trip you are about to take. Knowing where you want to go is just the start. You also need to understand your passengers, the car you are going to use, the weather, the time of day you are traveling, and when you need to arrive. Only after you understand all of these things can you look at a map and choose the streets and highways that will get you where you want to go.

You might ask whether online services such as MapQuest or Googlemaps have somehow changed all of this. I don't think they have. Once I print out directions from one of these services for my wife, the family navigator and chauffeur, she looks at them in light of the factors I mentioned in the previous paragraph. She often makes adjustments because of them—too much traffic at this hour, that highway is under construction, there are no streetlights on that road, or that particular road is very challenging when it is raining. Her goal is to get to the destination, but many things influence the route she takes to get there. She certainly doesn't choose the route before she knows where we are going and the factors that might influence our ability to get there successfully. However, when it comes to solving our customers' problems, that is exactly what we are prone to do.

For years, we have implemented technology-based learning solutions because we could. We believed what was said by the people trying to sell them to us or, even worse, the industry pundits who wanted to impress us with their knowledge of the newest, sexiest toys. In the old days (the 1980s and 1990s), we were lucky because there was usually only one or two new toys every few years. That's all changed. Over the past few years, we have encountered e-learning, mobile learning, virtual classrooms, blogs, Podcasts, and Wikis, just to name a few. (I am using a version of Microsoft Word with a copyright date of 2003, and neither blog nor Podcast even appears in spell check. What does that tell you about the pace of change?) If you add these new technologies to the dozens of media choices we had before, it's hard to know what to do.

Now you might say that this problem is limited to technology. I don't think it is. Have you ever given a client advice before you had all of the information you needed? Have you ever hired a consultant before you really knew what problem you were trying to solve? Have you tried a new delivery technique because you thought it might be fun without really thinking about its effect on learners? Have you ever jumped on the bandwagon because for no other reason than it was passing by and looked interesting? I have done all of these things, and I suspect many of you have, too. The question is what to do about it.

To me, the answer is simple. We must stop thinking about solutions first. We must resist the pressure or desire to choose what's new and interesting over that which is appropriate and useful. We must trust that our clients will prefer solutions that work to solutions that sizzle, and if they don't, we must help them understand the reasons why they should. In summary, we must believe in the various instructional design and consulting models that delay solution design until we thoroughly understand all facets of the business problem we are trying to solve, the audience for which the solution is intended, the context in which the solution will be delivered, and any other information that could influence the outcome. Only then will we be able to design or acquire solutions that will work and that will deliver the results our clients want and expect us to deliver.

We Must Become Educated, Discerning Consultants, Creators, and Consumers

Self-reflection is a terrible thing. Reflecting on the reasons you chose the subject matter for a book as you are writing the final paragraphs is a really terrible thing and potentially catastrophic. But, what I have come to realize is that my underlying frustration with the people who comprise our profession (myself included) is that we don't sufficiently educate ourselves about the things we need to know to do our jobs well. This failure causes us to make mistakes, to succumb to the lies about learning we encounter every single day.

The question is why this continues to happen, day after day, year after year. I think the reason is that we allow it to. We are so committed to helping our clients, to delivering products and services that are perceived as adding value, to be seen as making a meaningful contribution to the success of our employers that we are allow ourselves to believe things we probably shouldn't believe, which, in turn, causes us to do things we probably ought not to do. We don't rigorously analyze the claims of the vendors we talk to every day. We don't challenge conventional wisdom. We allow industry pundits to define the future for us and to tell us how we ought to cope with it. We've even let other

---

We must believe in the various instructional design and consulting models that delay solution design until we thoroughly understand all facets of the business problem we are trying to solve, the audience for which the solution is intended, the context in which the solution will be delivered, and any other information that could influence the outcome.

---

people make and act on judgments about the competencies required to do the work we do. Probably most significantly, we question the veracity of our own judgment each time we ignore that little voice in our heads that's telling us something isn't right.

So what do we do? I don't think there is an easy answer to that question. A good place to start is to apply one or two of the recommendations the authors provided in each of the chapters in this book. We also could remind each other every day that we are a profession and that we know some things that other people don't, even though they may think that this is not the case. Most important, we must start demanding more from the people with whom we work in support of our clients' needs—our partners, our suppliers, and, yes, ourselves. From others, we must demand more information, more ideas, more creativity, and, especially, more candor. From ourselves, we must demand more rigor. Simply, we must work harder to uncover the truths about learning that will free us to make the contributions we all want to make, that our clients expect us to make, and that, deep within ourselves, we know we are capable of making.

➤ About the Editor and Authors

The Editor

Larry Israelite

Larry Israelite has been involved in the field and of learning and development for more than 23 years. Currently, he is the director of human resource development at Liberty Mutual Group, where he focuses on enterprisewide learning initiatives in the areas of leadership and management, and professional skills. He also is responsible for the company's learning technology strategy and manages instructional product development. Prior to his position at Liberty Mutual, Israelite has held learning management positions at Pitney Bowes, the Forum Corporation, John Hancock Financial Services, Oxford Health Plans, and Digital Equipment Corporation. He holds a bachelor's degree from Washington College, as well as a master's degree in instructional media and a doctorate in educational technology, both from the Arizona State University.

The Authors (in Order of Appearance)

Murry Christensen

Murry Christensen has 20-plus years of experience in solving the people-process-technology equation. He is currently the principal of mchristensen.consulting, a consultancy in the technically enabled performance management field. Prior to becoming an independent consultant, Christensen built and managed the online learning group of Goldman, Sachs and Co., a global investment bank with more than 20,000 employees throughout the world. Earlier roles have included business development and solution design for a New York–based training and documentation consultancy; creating interactive training and marketing materials for major corporations in a range of industries; and working in the presentation, tradeshow, and meeting industries. He has founded and developed several advanced media production companies and maintains an active program of research, writing, and participation in learning industry associations. Christensen has presented at major industry conferences on a variety of topics. He has both bachelor's and master's degrees of arts from the University of Michigan and is a member of the Association for Computing Machinery (ACM-SIGGRAPH) and the Institute of Electrical and Electronics Engineers (IEEE) Computer Society.

Melinda Jackson

Melinda Jackson is the director of instructional design at Enspire Learning (http://www.enspire.com), an industry leader in custom e-learning and simulation development. She has more than 15 years' experience in project management and 13 years in instructional systems design. Formerly, she was project director of the Digital Media Collaboratory, a transdisciplinary research lab at the IC2 Institute of the University of Texas at Austin, whose mission is to research, to develop, to implement, and to study the impact and influence of new interactive technologies and digital content to enhance human performance and improve the social good. Jackson has presented widely on topics of games, simulations, and other interactive electronic environments for learning. She is published in books, journals, and magazines including *E-Learning Magazine, On the Horizon,* and the *Journal of Educational Computing Research.* She has led numerous instructional design projects for interactive, classroom, and blended curriculum and instruction. She received her master's degree in instructional technology from the University of Texas at Austin.

Beth Thomas

Beth Thomas is the executive vice president and chief learning officer for Sequent. She is responsible for leading Sequent's consulting practice, which includes the company's learning solutions consulting practice.

Thomas specializes in designing and leading transformational training. She has 20 years' experience helping organizations through major transformations, such as mergers and acquisitions and organizational change. Prior to joining Sequent, she was senior vice president and head of retail training development and planning at J.P. Morgan Chase. Before that, she worked at Limited Brands in Columbus, Ohio, where she created and managed the retailer's enterprise learning center and its service management practice. She has also worked for the international brokerage firm, the Fritz Companies. She is a frequent national speaker, and her professional work has been recognized with national awards and in several national-circulation magazines and newsletters. She has contributed to three books: *On-Demand Learning: Training in the New Millennium* by Darin Hartley (HRD Press, 2000), *Implementing e-Learning* by Lance Dublin and Jay Cross (ASTD Press, 2002), and Elliott Masie's *Learning Rants, Raves, and Reflections: A Collection of Passionate and Professional Perspectives* (Pfeiffer, 2005).

Len Sherman

Len Sherman is a senior lecturer at the College of Business Administration of Northeastern University where he teaches courses in business strategy. In addition, he serves as a senior business advisor to Accenture on a variety of strategy initiatives related to mergers and acquisitions and new business development. Sherman was the president of Accenture Procurement Solutions, a business process outsourcing business unit focused on delivering enterprisewide procurement services to businesses and government agencies. He also has served as interim president and strategy and business development lead for Accenture Learning. Sherman was a founding general partner of Accenture Technology Ventures, where he led Accenture's investment activities in supply chain management, procurement, and e-learning. Prior to holding these positions, he also led Accenture's global strategic services practice for a number of manufacturing based industries. Before joining Accenture, he worked at J.D. Power and Associates, where he had been managing partner of the firm's management consulting practice and Booz Allen Hamilton, where he was responsible for its U.S. automotive practice. Sherman has a bachelor's degree in aeronautical engineering, a master's degree in transportation systems, and a doctorate in transportation economics, all from the Massachusetts Institute of Technology.

Charlene J. Zeiberg

With more than 20 years' experience in adult learning, instructional design, and performance consulting, Zeiberg assists organizations in making the connection between strategy and business results: learning. She provides competency-based learning solutions aimed at providing employees with the essential skills that enable them to optimize their performance, transforming strategies into real results for her clients. She designs practical learning solutions along with specific organization development recommendations on how to eliminate factors hindering employees and managers from delivering measurable value. She has held corporate training positions with Fidelity Investments and Sun America and consulting positions with Andersen Consulting and The Forum Corporation. Before starting her own consulting practice, Zeiberg led the move to learning technology in her management role at PaineWebber. She earned a master's degree in human resource education from Boston University and a bachelor's degree in instructional design and technology from Ithaca College's Roy Park School of Communication and the Ithaca College London Centre.

Edward A. Trolley

Edward A. Trolley is widely recognized for having started the training outsourcing industry when he orchestrated the first comprehensive training outsourcing deal between DuPont and The Forum Corporation in 1993. After joining The Forum Corporation, he continued to advance the outsourcing concept with leading companies such as the Moore Corporation, NCR, Texas Instruments, KPMG Canada, SmithKline Beecham, Irving Oil, and other organizations around the globe. He has orchestrated more comprehensive training outsourcing relationships than anyone else on the planet. In 2002, Trolley was named as one of the "100 Superstars of HR Outsourcing" by *HRO Today* magazine. Trolley is co-author of the book, *Running Training Like a Business: Delivering Unmistakable Value* (Berrett-Koehler, 1999). He is a highly requested presenter at industry conferences and he has spoken at major events such as ASTD International Conference and Expo, TechLearn, the World Outsourcing Summit, and the HRO World Outsourcing Conference. His concepts and ideas have been included in hundreds of business publications around the globe.

Elliott Masie

Elliott Masie is an internationally recognized futurist, analyst, researcher, and humorist on the critical topics of technology, business, learning, and workplace productivity. He is the editor of *Learning TRENDS by Elliott Masie,* an Internet newsletter read by more than 56,000 business executives worldwide, and is a regular columnist in professional publications. He is the author of a dozen books, including *Learning: Rants, Raves, and Reflections: A Collection of Passionate and Professional Perspectives* (Pfeiffer, 2005) and the upcoming "Fingertip Knowledge" e-book. Masie is also leading a major research effort focused on Next Generation learning styles and Silver Generation workforce retention models. He heads The MASIE Center, a Saratoga Springs, New York, think tank focused on how organizations can support learning and knowledge within the workforce. He leads the Learning Consortium, a coalition of 331 *Fortune* 500 companies collaborating on the evolution of learning strategies, including WalMart, Target, United Parcel Service, the National Security Agency, BP International, Sears, Bank of America, and the U.S. Departments of Defense and Labor. Masie serves as an advisor to a wide range of government, educational, and nonprofit groups. He serves on the board of trustees of several colleges and on boards of national organizations. He serves as a pro bono advisor to the Department of Defense and was appointed by the president to the White House Advisory Council on Expanding Learning Opportunities.

J.P. Lacombe

J.P. Lacombe has 14 years of experience in the design, development, and implementation of learning technologies as a consultant in both the corporate and vendor environments. He has spent most of his career working with two notable vendors—SumTotal Systems and Pearson Performance Solutions—as he designed and implemented e-learning programs with *Fortune* 100 clients. He also spent time working as an in-house learning technologies and instructional design consultant for Aetna, John Hancock, and Fleet Financial Group (now Bank of America). He is currently working on building a leadership and organization development function at the University of Connecticut. Lacombe has taught learning technologies courses as an adjunct faculty member at Lesley College in Cambridge, Massachusetts, and the University of Massachusetts, Lowell. He holds a master's degree in instructional systems design from Florida State University and a bachelor's degree from the Newhouse School of Public Communications at Syracuse University.

Kerry Johnson

Kerry Johnson has 30 years' experience in the learning and consulting industries, the last 14 with The Forum Corporation where he is presently serving as an executive consultant. He has also served as The Forum's director of research and product development. Johnson has held several professorships, including at Syracuse University and the University of Maryland, where he also managed the Center for Instructional Design and Evaluation. He wrote with Lin Foa the book *Instructional Design: New Alternatives for Effective Education and Training* (American Council on Education, 1996), and he has written more than 40 book chapters, articles, and technical papers. His primary areas of expertise are the design and use of learning technology and the application of adult learning principles to leadership, teamwork, collaborative work processes, and knowledge management. His educational background includes a bachelor's degree in mathematics and physics from Gettysburg College, a master's degree in mathematics and psychology from the City University New York, and a doctorate in instructional design and evaluation from Syracuse University.

Steven P. Ober

Ober is an authority on leadership, executive team learning, and organizational change. He has worked successfully with senior executives in business, government, health care, and education. The focus of his work is helping individual executives, executive teams, and their organizations achieve outstanding business results, especially in the context of major change. Ober was a vice president at Arthur D. Little, a principal in Innovation Associates, and a member of the ADL Strategy and Organization Practice. He is the author of numerous articles and professional guidebooks, including "Achieving Breakthroughs in Executive Team Performance" (*Prism,* 1999), "Encouraging Enrollment: Personal Stories as a Vehicle for Change" (*Prism,* 2000), and "Cracking the Culture Nut: Human Systems Consulting" (Arthur D. Little/Innovation Associates, 2000). From 1994 to 2000, he led product development regarding team learning for Innovation Associates. The work resulted in a team-learning curriculum and a set of structured team consultations. In addition, Ober has conducted workshops on team and organizational learning at many national conferences. His focus at this time is supporting organizations involved in progressive social change, education, and the environment. He is known for his frankness, openness, honesty, and ability to unravel very difficult team and organizational problems.

David E. Stone

Stone is the owner and president of WorldWired, Inc., an international consulting practice focused on improving human performance. During 2004–2005, he was a visiting fellow in the Graduate School of Arts and Sciences at Harvard University. His work at Harvard has focused on the design of electronic performance support systems. During 2005–2006, he has been a visiting scholar at Harvard working on ethical issues associated with doing business globally. He is also a research fellow at the Massachusetts Institute of Technology where he is working with Eric Klopfer on applications of augmented reality to a variety of medical applications. Stone wrote with Constance Koskinen *Planning and Design for High-Tech Web-Based Training* (Artech House, 2002) and with Jan Potter *In Search of Perfect Performance* (Auerbach Publications, in press).

➤ Index